Tractate on a School Mount

by Alexander Nevzorov

bibliotheque

library

Tractate on a School Mount

Copyright ©2012 by Alexander Nevzorov

Photographs of Alexander Nevzorov
© Lydia Nevzorova

Published by Nevzorov Haute Ecole

www.hauteecole.ru

All rights reserved.

Printed in Charleston, S.C., United States of America.

No part of this book may be used or reproduced in any manner whatsoever without written permission except in the case of brief quotations embodied in critical articles and reviews.

First paperback edition published 2011.

ISBN 13: 978-5-904788-16-2

Project Head: Lydia Nevzorova
Managing Editor: Donna Condrey-Miller
Editor: Stasya Zolotova
Editorial Staff: Varvara Lyubovnaya, Cloe Lacroix,
Marie Duizidou
Art Director: Dmitri Raikin
Head of Pre-press Department: Eugene Mushtay

CONTENTS

Chapter 1
Superbia

The Secret Manuscripts of the School 5
Learning from Mistakes 11

Chapter 2
A Man on the Back

Understanding a Horse as an Exact Science 17
Confession 20
A Rider is "Blunt Object" 22
What Can Be Done? 24
The Blue Back 28

Chapter 3
The Main Question

Princeps Quaesitum 37
Frigusculum 43
"...Butt Devouring..." 50
Butt-mania 53

Chapter 4
The School Seat

1. Spatium 66
2. Interdictum 70
3. Magnitudo 76
4. Sella 83
5. Cordeo 84
6. Manege 87
7. Elements 90

SUPERBIA

Chapter One

The Secret Manuscripts of the School

I

There is an old half of a manuscript, half a book that, for the sake of brevity in the speech of the initiate, is referred to as "PRAECEPTIO PRECEPTORIBUS" (ill. 1).

The name of this very important treatise is actually much longer, "The Manual for Preceptors that Contains the Secret of Teaching of Horses According to the Wisdom of the School, and Dogma about the Importance of Keeping this Knowledge a Secret and also of Learning the Science of Superciliousness that is the Best Attitude for the Master of the School".

I am saying that it is "half a book, half a manuscript" because every PRAECEPTIO PRECEPTORIBUS manuscript has many written additions within its binding that were made at different times and by different authors who had direct connections with the School as well as to those spiritual movements that have given birth to the School.

This amazing and extremely rare half-manuscript was begun by an unknown author in the beginning of the seventeenth century.

It contains very mysterious and from time to time very ingenious instructions for teaching horses difficult elements, cabalistic mysteries and revelations, prophecies about the destiny of the horse and thoughts about the destiny of the earth after the death of the School masters.

A rule to strictly forbid spreading the PRAECEPTIO PRECEPTORIBUS has existed and was obeyed for at least two centuries.

On the fourth page of the book, it is explained in a highly categorical way: "This book, which must be written in by everyone who has the right to it, must not feel lead and become visible. If it is known that there has been a copy made, regardless of the importance of this person, according to protocol, the exact number of copies must be counted. Every copy greater than the third must be turned into well mixed ash."

5

Decoding the mysterious-looking phrases is very simple.

The phrase "must not feel lead and become visible" — is a simple indication of the inadmissibility of typographical printing, where, as it is well known, lead print was used for typesetting. Typography (of gravures and separate texts) could have been accomplished through threaded wooden print.

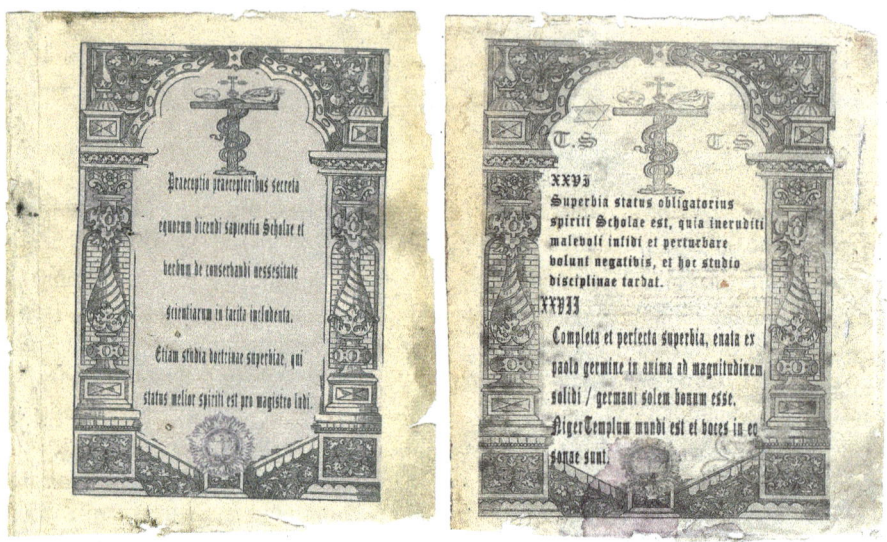

Ill. 1, 2. "PRAECEPTIO PRAECEPTORIBUS": Title page and page 100

The phrase "every copy greater than third… etc" is a direct instruction to destroy any surplus copies.

Many of what are called "Chinese copies" of "PREACEPTIO PRECEPTORIBUS" exist. As a rule, they are masonic manuscripts from the eighteenth to the nineteenth centuries.

These are less interesting.

Transcribers of these copies did not bother themselves with copying the long "horse" related chapters, limiting their copying only to those fragments where there were mystical or cabalistic revelations of the authors or "mystical Templar" exercises.

"Horse" related fragments exist in masonic manuscripts, but they have shrunken to a state of ugliness. Masonic manuscripts can easily be distinguished — there is a lot of "compass symbolism" in them, quite often to the detriment of the School, by the way.

So, as you have noticed even in the long title of the book, "the teaching of the science of superciliousness" is referred to.

II

As I have already said elsewhere, the negative meaning that the word superciliousness acquired in the Russian language [in Russian and English versions this word is related as arrogance] isn't consistent with the Latin meaning of the word SUPERBIA, which means "superciliousness" as well as "arrogance" and the precise translation of which is "over-existence" from the Latin SUPER (over) and from Sanskrit BHA (existence).

Even in Russian, by the way, if you think about the words arrogance (vesokomerie — высокомерие), and haughtiness (nadmennost' — надменность) they only mean "the use of the highest standard of measure" and "unwillingness to bargain, to be above barter".

In PRAECEPTIO PRECEPTORIBUS the teaching of "the science of superciliousness" takes up a good quarter of the manuscript. (Approximately 130 paragraphs). The importance of superciliousness and disdain for every other point of view is accentuated all the time. Extensively.

This is not the cultivation of arrogance, but teaching a person to use an amazing psychological instrument.

On approximately page 100 we find the 26th paragraph: "superciliousness is the indispensable state of the spirit of the School. Evil and insidious boors want to confuse us, to prevent us from seeing the truth and understanding the science" (ill. 2).

III

The skill to honestly disagree with those who do not hold a School-related point of view, the skill of not even considering them to deserve any attention, not even giving any respect for, or analysis of the opposing view — is a great skill that always gives beautiful results.

By the School's logic, the point of view of any opponent — is a priori considered to be idiocy. And this is very correct.

The existence of any other point of view about a horse — according to the general logic of this manuscript as well as the ideas of Pluvinel, and other great masters (preceptors of the School) — is a mere sign of brainlessness in the owner of this "other" point of view and a firm reason for refusing any further dialog with an opponent. And we have to follow, without fail, this masters' precept, a precept

7

of complete superciliousness and contempt for any other (aside from the School's) point of view.

The result of this practice over several centuries has shown that this way is extraordinarily constructive.

Besides, this practice makes a person completely psychologically resistant when it is fully implemented; this is what allows true progress in the area that we are interested in as well as allowing for true development of human characteristics.

Lord forbid Antoine de Pluvinelle listened to the points of view of his opponents or if he would have made some sort of alterations in his doctrine by allowing a compromise with the savagery and stupidity of the century.

Thank the gods Pluvinelle had perfectly mastered the spiritual practice of complete superciliousness and despised the accepted thoughts of his time regarding a horse in a splendid way. Historians who have noticed this trait thought it to be a personal quality of Pluvinell's character. But acquaintance with PRAECEPTIO PRECEPTORIBUS convinces us that SUPERBIA, above all, is a psychological skill that has to be mastered, made into an organic part of oneself and used in practice.

IV

What does this all lead to? It leads to talk about the mystery of the school seat.

For instance, there are several paragraphs in PRAECEPTIO PRECEPTORIBUS regarding a rider's seat. The most expressive of them is paragraph 83; in short it states, "the practice of dull riding, or repetitive exercises astride a horse's back, is extremely harmful to the strength and lightness of a true seat". This postulate is not outlined or discussed any further. The School superciliously designates the RULE. It is assumed that it will be followed without discussion.

From the view of a "horse-lover" in our days this rule is contrary from the beginning.

V

Let's look into it and once again collect evidence about the constructiveness of the School's superciliousness. The point of view that a good seat can only be formed by long "schooling" sessions, by hours spent in saddle, by long years of horseback riding exists today.

At some stage in time this standard point of view was proclaimed by the rider James Fillis, and has successfully been canonized and is universally recognized these days.

VI

Externally, this point of view looks logical and convincing. As it seems, there is nothing to argue about, but a simple and natural question arises: Why do those sportsmen (the very ones that work on their seat all the time) always fall off horses? (ill. 3a, 3b)

Everyone falls, not only the beginners –sport champions, students of sport champions, simple weekend riders and those that have their top degrees in riding.

Ill. 3a. Typical falling in sport. © G. Gavrilenko

They fall, traumatize, cripple, injure themselves and die. Sometimes they fall without any consequences, but everyone falls. During competition and trainings, in fields and parks, in deserts and riding arenas. They fall on expensive, well-drained footing, fall into ungroomed ravines, into pools and puddles and onto their own painted bars. Show jumpers fall, dressage riders fall, eventing riders fall, jockeys fall, etc.

Falls off a horse and equestrian sports are two undividable concepts — this does not require any proof.

9

VII

Why?

Any kind of training teaches a rider more about how to FALL than how to stay mounted. Any process of training consolidates negative experiences in a rider. Seemingly natural falls from lack of experience are changed into falls that are trained for.

It sounds paradoxical only at first glance.

Ill. 3b. Typical falling in sport. © G. Gavrilenko

Actually, this is a natural thing because it is well known that by practicing one's mistakes a person can do them automatically, making "making mistakes" one's style, which will inevitably lead to falls to the ground, and to funny crooks of the neck as well as other ridiculous and dangerous features of different equestrian sport seats.

The thesis of Abate Trittemia is very appropriate here: "This is the very case when long practice solidifies bad habits as well".

10

I repeat once more, that you can ignore this strange postulate and the fact that my views sometimes seem paradoxical, although ancient manuscripts support it. However, the amazing fallibility of sportsmen proves once again that the School's point of view is true.

Learning from Mistakes

VIII

Now, without being wicked, let's look at and analyze this "sad" consequence. This will help you to gain understanding of the most important principles of the School seat.

What can long schooling, hours spent in saddle, the practicing of dressage elements, jumping over painted bars, etc., teach?

They all teach a horse (who is in discomfort and pain) to resist and rebel, to catch any moment of weakness or unbalance of a rider in order to get rid of him by a means of a series of unpredictable, extreme movements. And they teach a rider to be afraid of a horse and its unpredictable movements.

This fear is an absolutely normal display of the self-preservation instinct, which creates very powerful automatic responses. Reflexive actions are being strengthened.

A rider's body learns to be afraid. He learns to tense up, be enslaved, grip on a horse, to respond with a spasmodic body stiffening to even the slightest hint of horse rebellion, almost with an entire body convulsion.

Finally, take a look at the faces of mounted sportsmen. If we cut the "swollen-head hat" off the head and delete the horse with the help of Photoshop, or cut the photos so that only the faces are left and show those faces to an objective observer with the question — "what are these people doing?" 90 % of the time, you will hear — "these people were photographed on the toilet, they've got constipation".

But this is true!

The other thing is that facial expressions do not only signal "constipation" but (aside from fear and anger) they signal extreme muscular tension in the entire body. The tension of a SEATED person*.

---

* Equestrian sportsmen are divided into two categories. The first ones sit astride as on a toilet seat, the second ones like they are impaled. Show jumpers, jockeys, cross-country riders are related to the first category. Dressage riders are part of the second category who also fall all the time, especially during schooling and while working young horses.

IX

Also, the more "experienced" the rider is, the stronger and more ingrained his reflexive response to any unexpected movement of a horse. The quicker the movement is, the greater the chance of falling. The connection between tensing and falling does not require any explanation, I hope.

X

And this is how it is in every training situation (regardless of the level of the trainer). Many negative skills, skills in the art of being afraid of quick and unpredictable equine movements, are being strengthened.

The skill of being afraid, the skill of being enslaved strengthens with every schooling ride. The rider's body does it automatically, regardless of any "cure" or psychological attitude. .

And this is natural! Until a horse is no longer perceived as a large, living piece of meat, whose emotions aren't clear, whose feelings and thoughts are hidden from a rider, until a horse no longer seems to a rider as something that needs to be broken, something which you can handle only with the help of a pain inflicting paralyzing tool in the mouth, or through the dull repetition of a conditioned response system of signals — there can exist no beautiful relationship between a horse and a rider, no matter which pretty words regarding "contact" are spoken. A horse is dangerous for a rider like this. A feeling of the danger of horses and horseback riding (H.R.) is always shown by the use of special and funny helmets — helmets that seem designed to make the sportsman's brain appear larger than it actually is, protective vests, and talks about some kind of safety rules.

Unhealthy conditions at horseback riding schools, where sportsmen with smashed-in faces due to a hoof kick roam freely, where those or other traumas happen every day. All of this subconsciously strengthens the fear of a horse that then will certainly appear while mounted, and will end in another fall and another trauma.

XI

To cut it short, until there is a "relationship" between a horse and human there is no true seat. The entire secret of a firm and light School seat is in the fact that this is the natural result of a right RELATIONSHIP between a horse and human. The basis of the School seat is an absolute absence of fear of a horse, understanding of its state, feelings and therefore — the horse's mood. There is a technique as well of course, but it has nothing in common with dull addition of hours in the saddle (moreover this addition of hours is absolutely contra-indicated.)

But we will speak about that a little later.

XII

The basis of the School seat is a relationship with a horse.

A horse is amazingly, devilishly clever, its intelligence is very alive, very "hot"; the horse has very good analytic abilities.

But what must be remembered at all times — a horse is a physiological being (like all mammals) and the basis for her feelings and behaviour, for her world-view are her physiological feelings. There is a very strong dependency on physi-ology–it makes a horse absolutely clear, logical and very consistent, after one has a full knowledge of horse physiology, of course.

XIII

How can a person know the response of a horse?

It is always ONLY the most straight and only logical answer to any question; it is al-ways a DIRECT reaction to any circumstance.

Of course, it is difficult to convert everything into horse concepts, having only a hu-man mind, but in the process of the work in hand and at liberty, this is something that ALWAYS happens. This is where it has to be remembered that the intelligence of a horse is almost the same as every other mammal, therefore is very much like a human.

But we must compare it to human intelligence without any additions of, so called, culture. i.e. without artificial layers like religious ideas or moral ideas or etiquette or social conventions and views that currently in many ways define the behavioural fea-tures of the animal we call "human".

XIV

I always explain to my students that the more they believe that the horse's mind is organic and full, the higher the results will be of the horse's education. This is the secret of the School and, as a consequence, of the School seat.

The first sign of relationship between a horse and human naturally is the removal of any metal or nasal means of control (ill. 4) *.

The School seat is a natural result of that full understanding. When the feelings and moods of a horse are clear and can be easily regulated at the "relationship" level, there is no need for any "pain inflicting" means of control.

---

* By nasal means of control we are referring to the side pull, hackamore, bosal, Parelli halter, etc., etc.

XV

It may be easily noticed that many horses are taking this step towards a human; they enable the rider to play a game called "Horseback Riding (H.R.)" — without metal.

Ill. 4. A true School seat is the most comfortable for the horse. Of course, it is only possible without "metal" in horse's mouth.

But this comes from the horse's merit, almost always. It is extremely clever. A rider, as a rule, ruins everything.

At times, a rider with so-called, "riding experience" takes off the metal or nasal means of control. But, unfortunately, this "riding experience" is only experience of negative character, and he tries to transfer the rules and habits of standard riding to relationship with a horse, without having mastered the skills of the School.

There is a habit of demanding, or ruling foolishly, to consider oneself the king and ruler, to whom a horse must obey. The poison of making demands of a horse already curses the blood of he who experiments, leading to imperious and very foolish demands.

These people have no understanding of spatium, they aren't used to complying with the interests of a horse, and understanding his pain and discomfort.

Another factor is activated as well. Riding "bitless" outside of the School is always uncollected riding, riding which is very primitive, ugly, and as destructive for a horse as riding with metal, as well as being extremely painful and mutilating the entire myological structure.

It all ends in a tragedy, which may be big or small, as can be expected. To simply take off the means of pain inflicting control and to dabble about on horseback can be done by absolutely anyone.

To perform very difficult elements, to have control over a horse's spirit — without any means of external control is something only the School knows how to do.

A MAN ON THE BACK

Chapter Two

Understanding a Horse as an Exact Science

I

One hundred percent of a horse's feelings have absolutely precise physiological, biomechanical, myological, psychological and other characteristics that can be understood by man.

Thank the gods, everything is known. Everything is more or less clear.

II

The School mount of a rider, which is the topic of our conversation, is developed from an exact knowledge of a horse's feelings about a man being on its back, and from a desire to minimize the harm and discomfort that a rider always brings to the horse.

I'll explain now that presence of a man on the horse's back never gives a horse any pleasant feelings. Without any regard to whom that human is. It makes no difference. It may be a refined riding master of the Royal Riding School of Vienna, who has been polishing his mount for thirty years, a thoughtless person who rents a horse, a showjumping rider who finds a special pleasure in torturing a horse, or a conscientious Natural Horsemanship student who consciously doesn't want to "abuse a horse". I reiterate that this doesn't matter.

The physiological feelings stemming from the myological system of the horse's back, dermis and epidermis, are nearly all the same. It sounds paradoxical, but I will further clarify and explain this postulate.

III

The way to calculate a horse's feelings is quite simple.

In all cases the same laws of physiology apply, according to which the soft tissues of the back and the main skeletal and subdermal muscles undergo compression and this

17

always causes physiologically-based negative feelings or sensations, from discomfort to pain. Feeling pleasure from discomfort or pain isn't an attribute of any living being.

IV

> If riding on horseback gave the rider all the painful feelings that the rider brings to the horse, I can tell you that horseback riding as a historical entity wouldn't exist. Man would just anathematize the horse.

V

Any talk about "love" that a horse has for being ridden, "trail rides", or "pleasure riding", or in general, to the presence of a man on its back, is a very funny dilettantism.

It is a very vulgar and absolutely blind substitution of reality by what is desired. It is the substitution of a very convenient stereotype for the truth.

This stereotype is propagated by what I would call a "mucky girl." *

Weak-minded and hypnotized by so-called "equestrian experts", they repeat this rubbish with different degrees of ecstasy and persuasion.

It is interesting that the irony of saying that any other creature "loves" when somebody sits on its back, batters at the muscles and the spine with all his weight and compresses the living tissues on its back does not come to anybody's mind. This effect is always uncomfortable for any living tissue.

VI

Panegyrics of horseback riding within equestrian circles is sometimes an attempt to justify a personal desire to entertain, but more often, it is a slavish, unthinking dependency on stereotypes.

Taking into account the low intellect of equestrians it is no surprise. Statements like "horses love equestrian sport" sound even funnier, or the thought that the horse is "happy" under the rider.

In order to prove such statements a whole set of complicated experiments would be needed to show that some horses must be masochists, which means they gain pleasure from physiological discomfort or pain.

---

* A «mucky girl» is and the term for girls of varying ages who work with horses without any basis of hippological or scientific knowledge about the horse. They smoke, drink, use slang, beat horses with whips and use the phenomenon of NCS (neurocranial shock) brought about by the use of bits to control the horse.

Such experiments haven't been conducted; there is no scientific proof that a horse with a masochistic mind exists.

VII

The concept that a person sitting on a horse's back brings with it some kind of "pleasure" is a dense misunderstanding of the main principles of a horse's myology and physiology and all the principles of elementary physiology of mammals in general.

It is an absolute and PRINCIPLE ignorance of the horse.

VIII

However, sportsmen cannot admit to weakmindedness, and they are doomed to ignorance.

Their relationship with a horse is based only on strong painful impact. The horse's feelings, in fact, do not worry, have never worried and shouldn't worry them. The process of raping, as we know it, doesn't assume even the slightest interest in the feelings of the person being raped (or only of an increase in the pleasure of the rapist from the sufferings that are caused).

As soon as the truth about the relationship between a man and a horse becomes known, equestrian sport ends. Ignorance is its only cause.

IX

I feel like I can speak out bravely. Sportsmen, even if they began reading this tractate, are already asleep.

Their small and regularly-perspiring-under-a-helmet-or-top-hat brain refuses to perceive the text, everything distorts and mixes-up.

This is excellent. We can now speak calmly and openly.

So, horseback riding, the human presence on top on the horse's back, until now has been an important School discipline.

Yes, the proportion of the studies "from the ground", "in hand", or "at liberty" to the studies "under saddle" is nearly 90 percent to 10 percent, but these 10 percent exist. Maybe the next, even more honest and more enlightened generations will perceive this discipline (riding) as barbarism and perversion, but for the present moment, as I have already said, it exists. Yes, Nevzorov Haute Ecole has a rather high goal and absolutely honorable methods. It seems that we are completely different from sportsmen.

However, as I have already mentioned, there is the matter of the soft tissues of the horse's back, which is the reason for discomfort or pain.

19

Confession

X

Let's frankly confess that the Nevzorov Haute Ecole rider, when on horseback, in principle, can bring to the horse the same unpleasant physiological feelings as an alcoholic show-jumper. I assure you, the endomysium or perimysium of the muscle experiences compression and distress, which translates to discomfort or pain.

The title, degree, and intentions of a rider aren't important.

The horse doesn't care if this discomfort comes from the desire to just stupidly "pleasure ride", jump over painted bars or from the fine intention to rehearse a difficult element.

This confession is a turning point, an incredibly important moment. But even its sincerity should be based on absolute knowledge.

XI

What happens inside a horse's back?

An average TOTAL surface area of the panels of the saddle that contact the horse is about 300–500 cm^2. But this is the total area; let's not fool ourselves.

We can and we must speak only about the surface area of the strongest pressure, i.e. about those miserable 50 cm^2, that have the most influence on the horses' back. An average rider's weight is 70 kilograms (154 pounds). The pressure for 1 cm^2 of the horse's back is about 1 kilogram, 300 grams per cm^2. This figure can vary from 1 to 1.5 kilos (2.2 to 3.3 pounds).

What does this figure mean?

XII

This figure means, that with a saddle perfectly fitted to the specific horse's back, with an ideal, "glued" School seat on the soft tissues of the back, and to be precise, on the tissues of the transversospinal muscles, the trapezius muscle, the tissues of the longissimus muscle, the epidermis and dermis which is filled with sensitive receptors, on all of these structures we have a pressure, on average, of 1.5 kilos (3.3 pounds) per square centimeter.

Take a bar weighing 1.5 kilograms, with an end that has the surface area of one square centimeter and put it on your back, near the spine, asking somebody to hold it so it doesn't fall, but let it rest on your back vertically. Imagine that there are 50 points of pressure like this — united or not. And that's not all.

The average weight of a saddle is about 5 kilos (11 pounds).

This is if you just rest it on the back, not tightening the girth.

And if the girth is tightened? How many times will the pressure increase? Not the weight, but the force of pressure on the horse's back?

There is a simple School example done with a string, which can explain a lot (ill. 5).

We take a simple scale. It should tell us approximately what horse feels.

We put a common leather string on the scale.

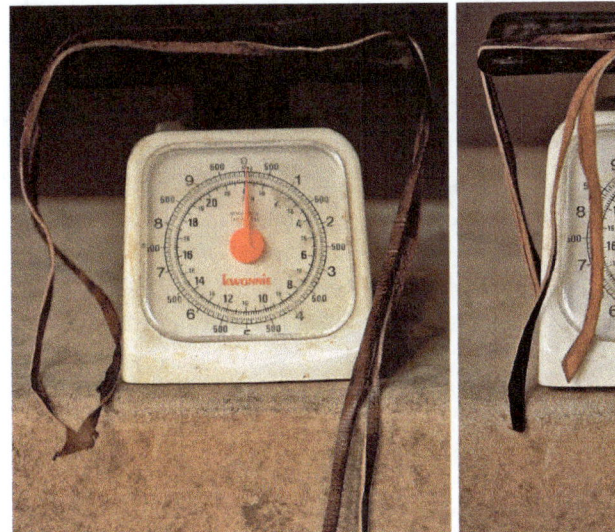

Ill. 5. School example with a string: by itself (left); tying like a girth (right). © Nevzorov Haute Ecole

By itself it weighs about three grams.

Now we tie it like a girth around the scale, not very tightly.

Now the scale feels the string like it's something that weighs 4 kilos (8.8 pounds). Its weight has essentially been multiplied.

A "crushing" effect between two objects took place.

A horse's back experiences the same thing that our scale does. Compressed between the drawn-tight girth and the panels of the saddle, it feels the multiplied saddle pressure, which seemingly weighs just 5 kilos.

We must add this multiplied saddle weight to the rider's weight and talk about the aggregation of impact on soft tissues of the back by these TWO factors. In total,

21

we get a pressure of not less than 3 kilos (6.6 pounds) per square centimeter of the horse's back.

This is already a serious problem.

A Rider is "Blunt Object"

XIII

And now honestly and in detail we shall examine the physiological effect and therefore the feelings of a horse.

The formula of "trauma by blunt object" is well known in forensic science. Ironically and bitterly, it is this formula that shows the most complete and the most honest way of characterizing our situation.

The rider himself is the "blunt object". It is a sad and funny conclusion after many thousands of years of riding.

The presence of a man on the horse's back can only be considered a "traumagenic" factor and not in any other way.

Moreover, in our case we must speak about so-called "combined" trauma, due to the damage of the anatomical structures of tissues that happens in multiple areas.

The extreme result of the presence of a saddle, girth and rider can be seen in the photo (ill. 6). But these are extreme, criminal results.

XIV

These extreme results enable us to confidently say that a saddle and a rider, in essence, are creating that traumagenic situation.

> **Of course, there are stages, but if the end result of the impact is a deep trauma and destruction of skin and some of the muscles, then the beginning and intermediate stages are discomfort and pain.**
> **This is a law of traumatology.**

XV

Most saddles have a hard wood, fiberglass, plastic, or metal tree.

Its effect in addition to the rider's weight and the impact of the shifting of this weight will always, no matter what, accompany all of a horse's movements regardless of saddle stuffing, pads, sweat flaps, etc.

22

XVI

Forensic examination classifies impact of this type as "compression, friction, crushing of organs and tissues, global or local graze wounds."

I shall repeat, horrible photos are shown only as an example of the logical completion of the type of impact we are studying.

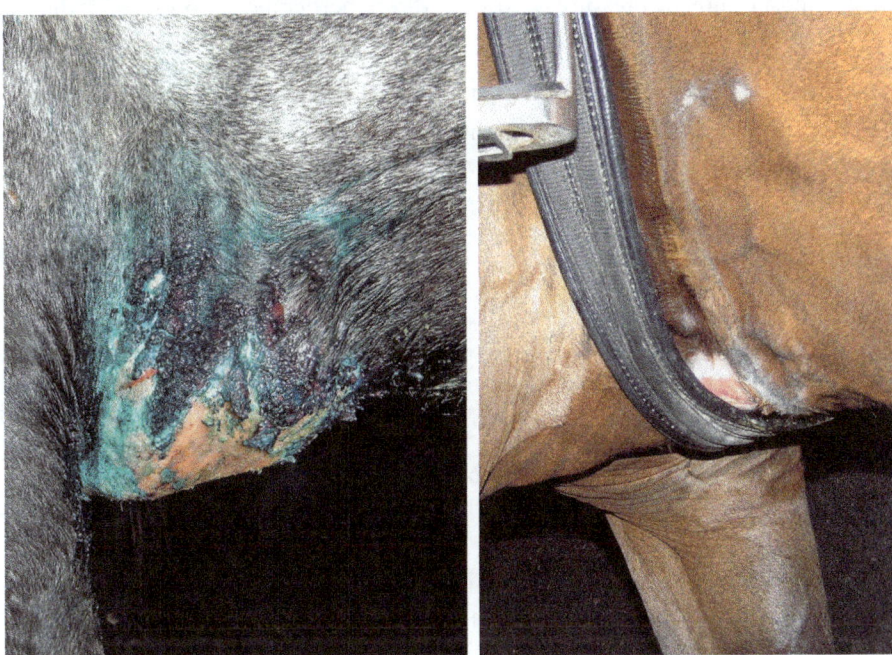

Ill. 6. Extreme traumas from saddle, girth and rider. © Nevzorov Haute Ecole, S. Spartantseva

We won't speak about such deep trauma. We are not touching the area of terrible traumas, we are only talking about discomfort and pain as the first stages of the impact that leads to similar traumas.

XVII

So, on to trauma by blunt object.

I'm quoting a typical forensic textbook:

1. Practically every object that is in prolonged forceful contact with the skin or muscles of any living being damages them to one degree or another.

2. Pressure is a prolonged forceful interaction of an object and body tissues.

23

3. The exterior sign of pressure is an appreciable or significant impression in relief of an object's traumatizing surface.

   In criminal cases that is, for example, an imprint of a tyre tread or the bars of a radiator on a person who has been hit by a car. In our case, it is the impression of a saddle pad.

4. The most traumatic pressure is "straight, direct, perpendicular pressure" (which is exactly our case).

One more sign of pressure is sweat production in the area under pressure.

We can see both; saddle pad impression and sweat production under the saddle on a horse. All are signs of pressure.

The effects of AA (aggressive action) on live tissues are in front of us.

Take note!

The tissues that suffer the most and are exposed to microtraumas are the transversospinal muscle tissues…

It seems they are hidden more deeply, but the fascicles of their fibers run from the spinous processes behind the vertebrae, to the mastoids which lie afore, which makes them especially vulnerable to pressure from above simply because of their location.

> **In short, we have a scientifically proven fact, which allows us to state that not a single horse feels pleasure from a rider being on his back.**
>
> **That is the sad physiological truth.**
>
> **All the discussions from riders and their "feelings" about what a horse experiences under the saddle — are strained feelings, self-deception, fantasies and ignorance.**

What Can Be Done?

XVIII

Is it possible to minimize uncomfortable (I do not even speak about painful) feelings of a horse? It is.

This is where a Nevzorov Haute Ecole Master differs from the dilettante-sportsman who climbs up on a horse.

He must be aware of what a horse feels when a person is on his back.

When the methods of painful control disappear and a man refuses to control by means of a "pain hypnosis" in the form of metal and kilometers (miles) of straps —

and everything is based on "relationship" — the necessity to know exactly what a horse is feeling becomes critical so as not to spoil and compromise these relations.

For a sportsman, in view of his stupid ways of controlling the horse, this is unnecessary and absolutely uninteresting.

XIX

I repeat one more time: for the School seat, a principle understanding and clear knowledge of all myological features and physiological processes which take place in the back of a horse when a man is astride is a prerequisite.

We can do nothing with the fact that a man on horseback causes a horse at least some discomfort.

XX

Muscles have the right to have their say. Moreover, this voice of the horse is more authoritative than man's vote.

It's an entity, and we have to heed it. And we must listen to this voice with all its distinctions, with all its variations.

Our task is to know this problem and to try to minimize it.

XXI

If we have gradual AA (aggressive action) on tissues, which has as its end result a severe trauma, it would be natural to divide or categorize the way from completely sound tissues to traumatized tissues into several stages.

XXII

Let's mark the first stage as lack of specific sensations, the second stage — discomfort, the third — pain, and the fourth — trauma.

We may not even think about causing trauma or even pain, our goal is not to cross the line from "lack of specific sensations" to simple discomfort.

For this a person ought to:

1. Know exactly the time allowed for us to be on horseback.

The feeling of discomfort (caused by microtraumas to the tissues) doesn't appear right away, this is confirmed by research..

25

2. Know the circumstances that signal the beginning of sensations of discomfort for a horse.

3. Know the circumstances that "minimize discomfort", i.e. those that postpone the beginning of sensations of discomfort.

XXIII

A simple analysis of "when I do what I do — what does she feel" is the shortest way to a horses' heart and to a fantastic effectiveness in the education of a horse.

But the question "What does she feel?" we should answer honestly. Extremely honestly. And from the honesty of this answer, "horse lovers" and sportsmen are running as if from the plague. They hide from even the simplest knowledge.

XXIV

Even now they are making up a myriad of excuses like "I have a very expensive saddle, it can't be uncomfortable", "I have an extraordinary butt, I do special fitness exercises", "I have the world's best coach, special riding breeches, — and I'm fed up with your physiology and anatomy, get out of here, my horse loves when I ride him, he recognizes me".

All of this and similar balderdash in the style of "mucky girls".

I'll tell you directly: neither saddle price, nor features of butt construction and composition, nor breech cut, have any neutralizing or advantageous outcomes when it comes to physiology and anatomy.

XXV

The more strictly the rider questions himself, the more full and precise his image of the physiological sensations that the horse experiences, the more honestly he can answer himself, and the more effective the educational process is.

But, as I have already mentioned, in order to answer honestly you must understand.

My apologies for my harsh attitude, but I am repeating again and again, that the understanding of the physiological sensations of a horse with all their nuances is vitally important.

The person who doesn't understand this "physiological grammar", doesn't understand a horse, doesn't understand anything.

All that has to be done is to simply think, to break out of the stereotype and to think. Then many things will become possible.

Investigations into the deep psychology of a horse, different kinds of "extra-sensory", or shamanistic practices are not the foremost things.

They are attractive and may be extremely necessary in the School work with a horse, but everything arises first from physiology and anatomy.

> **You can learn by heart the teachings of Pluvinel and Fiachi, you can string yourself from head to toe with Lakota amulets, you can learn all the charms of Falling Coyote or "Horse Encyclopedia", but if you simply cause a horse pain or discomfort, she won't make friends with you.**

XXVI

Idiotic entertainment which they call equestrian sport cannot bear coming to any scientific or serious veterinary understanding and therefore, does not perceive any arguments.

Ill. 7. A harmful seat. © S. Spartantseva, G. Gavrilenko

This means that the School interdicts do not spread to voluntary cretins.

Firstly, they need to satisfy their "itch" that makes them climb up on to their poor horses.

27

This severe "itch" in the denoted parts of the body is always much more important to them than any facts of science, veterinary knowledge and sense.

They do not worry much about the fact that they, with the help of their sport, will kill the horse.

The itch worries them much more. The victims of this itch which makes people forget everything can be found in both adults and children.

All efforts to educate them are equal to the efforts to wean Koreans of eating dogs (ill. 7).

Ill. 8. Singular sportsmen's argument. © HorseRacingKills.org

Any efforts to prove the idiotic essence of their entertainment, the science, the veterinary knowledge, the School, this public answer… they fight against with their one obscene and insensately argued point (ill. 8).

The Blue Back

XXVII

Actually, it isn't blue; the colour is closer to turquoise.

However, out of consideration for the international thermographic term Venetum Dorsum we may continue calling it blue.

Only the "blue back" (ill. 9a) can serve as a real and definitive sign that a horse has no discomfort, pain or soreness, whether it be new, chronic, local or global.

The blue back is an absolute ideal and should be considered an absolute norm. [*]

Only the presence of the blue back can offer us this assurance.

Only when there is Venetum Dorsum can the weight of the rider, or any pressures (the saddle and the rider) not be considered a torture to the horse.

Everything is so simple.

Everything is easy to explain, easy to prove and easy to understand.

A horse's body is an exact science.

You can diagnose the blueness of the back in two ways.

The first method (relatively complicated) is a computer thermograph.

XXVIII

A computer thermograph is a complicated instrument that locates all the areas of inflammation in the horse's body. (Right now, we are talking about the back).

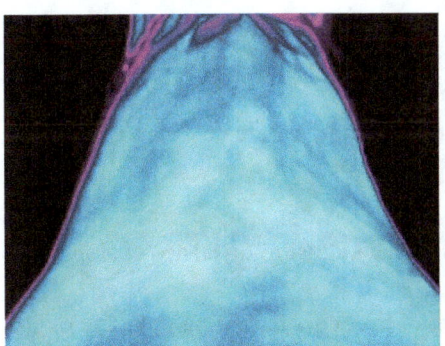 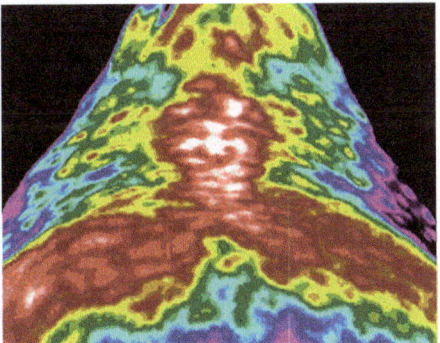

Ill. 9a — back of an absolutely sound horse (left); 9b — a show jumper (right)

Deep inflammation or spinal injuries are shown in a certain way; inflammation of the derma or epidermis in another way, and superficial and deep muscles injuries in yet a third way. The point is that all inflammation is clearly shown.

---

[*] "The blue back" showed on the thermogram is the back of the same stallion that you can see on practically all of the illustrations of the Tractate. And that, is that.

29

Any purple, red or orange marks indicate only one thing: there is inflammation due to trauma or destructive processes and therefore there is strong pain in that place.

Here's a simple example.

On the thermograms (ill. 9b, 9c, 9d) there are examples showing the back of three very different sport horses. The first one, if I'm not mistaken, is a showjumping horse of the highest level, the second and the third ones are dressage horses.

All of these horses are out of good health. All of them suffer, some worse than the others. The damage ranges from painful trauma to chronic back injury.

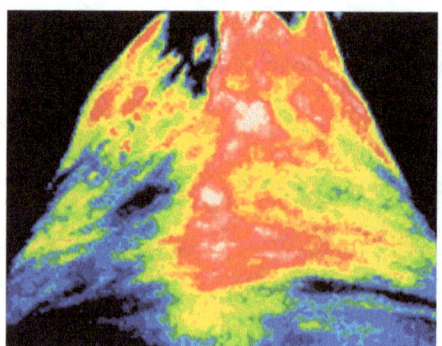 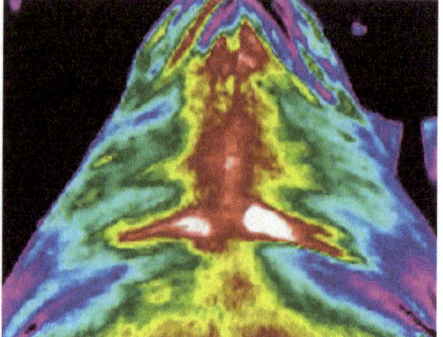

Ill. 9c–d — dressage horse backs

It is interesting that the owners of all three horses had no idea that their horses were seriously ill, and they larked around with them (and still do!) to what they call "the max" (training, taking part in competitions, etc.).

The three backs are very typical. In equestrian sport, there are no other backs.

XXIX

Maybe these images serve as a kind of a mirage, illusion or falsity of a spurious device.

On the other hand, maybe it is the fantasies of the School, wanting to justify its "incredibly strict" SPATIUM and interdicts.

No. The severe back injuries of all sport horses are scientifically proven fact.

Let's take a paradigmatic academic edition, which has the status of a textbook, it is called "Principles and Practice of Equestrian Sport Medicine" and is under the editorship of D.R. Hodson and R.J. Rose. Open to the eighth chapter; "Myological Anatomy, Physiology and Adaptation toTraining Exercises", which was written in association with professors of veterinary medicine, David Shaw (Australia) and Stephany Yalberg (USA).

What shall we see?

Bah! We'll see a terrible (but so well known) list of typical myopathies, the first of them, (from an inner crush injury) destruction of muscular tissues which is caused by the leaking of myoglobine and other contents of the cells (including creatine, kinase, and aldolase) into the blood-vascular system, and mitochondrial myopathy.

As a standard problem, we'll see the crushing of the *permisium*, affectation of the *endomisium* and the *epimisium*, and therefore there will be spasmodic myotonia.

The trauma of inner bursting of muscular tissue (transverse bursting of course) is described as a typical one. This fact, which is delicately not announced by the School — which doesn't want to pile on the pressure, is clearly described by the veterinary sports textbooks.

What I refer to is strong necrosis of skeletal muscles.

However, I will have to return to the necrosis of skeletal muscles as a result of forced collection.

What is interdicted by the School is, as it turns out, known by sports medicine. The difference is that the School, from the very beginning, liquidates the reason for the problem. The sports veterinary industry sadly only attempts to cure the outcomes by deducing how severe the necrosis of the muscle is, observing how the inner fibrotic tissues are forming etc.

The School interdicts, readings from a diagnostic computer and the scientific facts of veterinary medicine, as you can see, say 100 percent the same thing. (Who would have had any doubts?)

In other words, when we say "sport horse", we say "invalid horse". This is about equestrian sport of all levels, from horse for hire to the Olympics.

I have already mentioned that the owners of the three horses whose thermograms were shown as examples of strong pathology were absolutely sure that their horses were healthy.

Sounds strange, doesn't it?

In this case, one really sad factor appears; when the pain becomes chronic, the horse physiologically understands that any opposition leads to much more pain than so-called obedience, and he will compliantly perform the showjumping or dressage patterns.

In addition, the horse has exact physiological and mycological knowledge that any opposition will lead to exacerbation of the impacts of the bit on the nerves of the head,

31

and the deep boring impacts on these nerves will effectively make a final mess of all his biomechanical construction and redouble the sufferings in the whole body.

XXX

Moreover, the equestrian sport practice uses "the traumatic calm" of a horse, however strange it may sound.

Brazenfaced, Salomon de la Broue wrote honestly about it.

A couple of century's later, Prussian and German theorists of cavalry repeat after de la Broue, "Only after something hurts the horse — he becomes truly obedient".

In fact, usually only serious inner injuries and pathologies give complete power to a rider.

The nature of every trauma and of every pathology is that its chronic, smoldering state is less painful than the outbreak of pain that is unavoidable while opposing the rider.

XXXI

Only when the pain itself becomes excessive and reaches a lasting apogee in the so-called work, does the horse decide to commit mutiny, physiologically realizing that the highest point of pain has already been reached, and although there is little hope to escape the creature who is torturing him, hope exists and it is worth chancing (ill. 10).

Well, honestly, I didn't want to show it so as not to offend an extra sensitive reader too much, but I'm afraid I have to.

Here is the photo of the autopsy (ill. 11) of a horse that was considered healthy, myologically at least.

On the photos, you can easily see the affected regions.

This is necrosis of the skeletal muscles which were mentioned above, and which the veterinary sports folios decree as being the most typical condition to diagnose.

XXXII

In this case, we see a very severe, obvious and definite chronic affectation of the splenius neck muscles. The ones that together with the trapezius and atlas muscles — suffer most of all from forced collection.

The grey mass that is perfectly seen and shown in the picture is unquestionably necrotized muscle tissue.

Ill. 10. "Traumatic" calming of the horse. © G. Gavrilenko, A. Davidova

Dead muscle tissue within the body of the living horse whom the equestrian sport community foredoomed to be a "happy athlete" (It is phenomenal that this term be used by the FEI in such an instance of marasmus. The term "happy athlete" is used for dressage horses.)

XXXIII

However, let's get back to our topic.

First, let's move from the neck to the back, the topic of our discussion today.

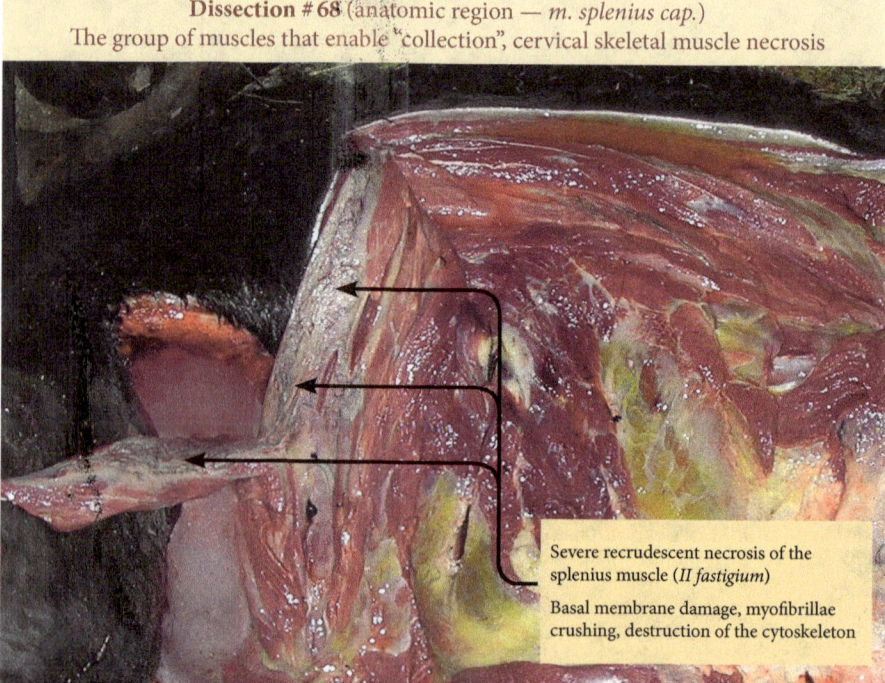

Dissection # 68 (anatomic region — *m. splenius cap.*)
The group of muscles that enable "collection", cervical skeletal muscle necrosis

Severe recrudescent necrosis of the splenius muscle (*II fastigium*)

Basal membrane damage, myofibrillae crushing, destruction of the cytoskeleton

Ill. 11. © Nevzorov Haute Ecole

The thermographic examination is an absolute and accurate method of diagnosing damage.

XXXIV

Another method of diagnostics, absolutely faultless, consists of the simple knowledge that the rider broke the School interdicts and spatium.

Unfortunately, any infractions of the interdicts or spatium will always, and definitely, cause the strongest, pathological and irreversible outcomes in the myological condition of the horse.

If the interdicts and spatium are maintained, we can be absolutely sure about avoiding strong damage or other myological pathologies (myopathies).

XXXV

Eitherway, I'll speak of the Interdicts and Spatium in the last chapter of the "Treatise", so I don't think it is suitable to speak of them now. After all, they are only a School matter, others, who are wallowing in their sport mediocricy, would still mutiliate and kill horses.

THE MAIN QUESTION

Chapter Three

Princeps Quaesitum

I

So, the PRINCEPS QUAESITUM (main question) still exists.

It sounds very unpleasant, it perplexes and makes one angry but it will not go away and it remains the primary question if we are concerned with the art of riding and the authenticity of the School seat. The true School seat can only begin from an honest answer.

> **This question is simply, "Why? What is the purpose of you being astride?"**
>
> **This is the key question, the answer to which contains everything to do with the relationship, as a box contains precious jewels. It is the big picture. This is also the touchstone by which everything else is judged, and in the case of a correct answer, this is the key to the true School seat.**

II

We shall not comment on equestrian sport bullshit propaganda about the necessity of working a horse in order to avoid muscle dystrophy* or the riding-masters' confident belief in the necessity of horses "earning their keep".

Of course, we also aren't discussing this as an alternative source to equestrian sport amusement or so called "training", or for pleasure riding, that method of the horse hauling a person's idle-ass around.

These pastimes are for weak-minded people who have no equine knowledge and therefore must be read about in some magazine. Their answers are worthless for us.

> **However, sometimes weak-minded and ignorant people are entertaining and can show us what not to do and help us to better understand the essence of the question.**

---

* True myological-based education of a horse, the development of MAGNITUDO (power and freedom) is possible only in hand at liberty. There are several groups of School exercises that gymnasticize a horse this way.

37

III

To compete in equestrian sports or for pleasure riding nothing is required but ignorance, a desire for self-aggrandizement or a desire to gain pleasure from actions that cause a horse pain.

When the scientific proof of the damage of equestrian sports is gathered together, we can see a simple truth emerge.

It is important to understand that in classical riding as in equestrian sports there is no relationship between a horse and human, nor is there mastership, nor art.

There are however, quite a number of primitive, pain inflicting skills and rules regarding their application. Anyone can master these skills if they are the least bit cruel and ignorant. So, the low IQ of everyone practicing any type of equestrian sports should not cause us even the slightest surprise.

These people naturally cannot ask the question "Why?"

A horse's back for them is something you ought to sit on.

It is "the place where the butt is placed".

It is what you need to climb onto for relaxation or pleasure.

Of course understanding the subtleties of the horse's neurological and anatomical properties or studying the myological characteristics of this "place to put a butt" in this type of community will never come to mind.

They are only concerned with the comfort of their butt.

For instance, the simple and absolutely innocent remark that they are placing their butt on the brain of a living creature, is at first surprising for them and then it will bring them to a rage, guaranteed.

IV

Although it is clear even to a fool that the *medulla spinalis* (spinal cord brain) — is exactly the same brain as the cerebrum and *medulla oblongata* and has exactly the same complicated functions but is more vulnerable because of the absence of a stable and permanent protective capsule (the skull) that contains the *cerebrum*.

V

It is useless to explain anything to them. They will never understand nor accept it. According to Zen, these are the sort of people who "have no cup".

VI

By "have no cup" I am referring to the well-known story about a Zen master and a foolish lay brother.

"When the foolish lay brother asked his master a difficult question about destiny, the master answered: 'I can answer your question but will not because you will not understand it. Imagine that I have a teapot with tea and you want to drink. I am ready to give you tea, but you need a cup. You haven't got one. If I pour tea into your fists, you will get burned and will scream in pain. We will ruin your fists, the mats and the varnish on the floor... and you will not even get to taste it'".

In exactly the same way, this knowledge is useless for "horse-lovers". By getting it they will burn their fists and scream from pain but the taste of knowledge will be unknown for them because they "have no cup". The taste of knowledge is only truly understood through application.

For those who want to understand the School seat I would recommend to learn well this Zen story as well as the great rule of SUPERBIA, in the light of which any arguments of those who are against the School are regarded as what they really are — complete nonsense.

What do I mean by "a cup"? By a cup, first of all, I mean the love of a horse, but not the equestrian ass-riding love that is identical to the love of a "biker" for his bike or moped.

But the true love that feeds on the knowledge of a horse and that drives one to know precisely the feelings and sensations of the one you love and to put their well being above your comfort and caprices.

VII

Not everything is clear at the very beginning, not all of our senses tell the truth.

Stereotypes are a strong influence, they may be more comfortable even if they are false but they should never be substituted for the truth. It is necessary to have absolute anatomical and physiological knowledge of the horse.

These scientific disciplines are merciless, astute, almighty, and will never allow the truth about the sensations of a horse to be replaced by a comfortable or attractive lie.

VIII

But we must return to our main question, to the PRINCEPS QUAESITUM.

In the second chapter of this "Tractate" I have already explained that a horse's back is a very tender, highly sensitive and very fragile part of a horse's body.

But there I was only talking about the simple, strictly myological problems having to do with compromised circulation in the blood vessels in the muscles of the horse's back under the crushing vertical pressure of a rider's weight.

If we're honest then these consequences (although they torture and disfigure a horse without a doubt) are very innocuous ones.

The School seat begins from infinite respect for the horse's back. In our case this respect is for our own benefit and is absolutely not built on blind worship of the horse.

IX

Actually, any blind worship, be it to Odin, be it to a horse, to Aphina, or to Jesus, is idiotic in its essence. And there is no place for an idiot on horseback.

X

We must analyze and understand the sensations of a horse perfectly.

When I am talking about "our own benefit" I mean our need to establish and preserve our relationship with a horse.

A horse, like all mammals, is strictly physiological and the relationship to the world (and a human) is based first of all on physiological sensations. For the establishment and preservation of these relationships at first it is only required that we simply not cause any pain or discomfort. It is not the horse but we who need these relationships; therefore we are speaking about our own benefits.

XI

Actually, humankind is a very interesting community.

History shows us that there has always been an extraordinarily strong fascination with having a "special relationship with a horse".

These special relationships were thought to be hidden in mysterious practices like Shamanism, available only to a few people with special powers.

It is enough to glance at antique hippological works to find a mass of recipes for such sorts of relationships.

For example, Gothic French texts instruct that in order to obtain power over a stallion, one must cut out the heart of a hanged man, clean and tan it, and make it into a wallet. Into this tanned heart at the right moment one had to add lead shavings, powdered gold, human and horse blood, mix it all under the light of three torches with a finger cut from the same hanged man, and then to hang this "wallet" around one's neck.

This would guarantee the owner of this wallet good relations with a stallion during shoeing, grooming and breaking in.

The "power of a horse" has been a dream and delusion. Hundreds of manuscripts were written, books that contained phenomenal recipes for such relationships were printed.

Of course these recipes have nothing in common with the School. The School Masters saw it all as the work of amateurs; nevertheless these recipes were in high demand beyond the ideological walls of the School.

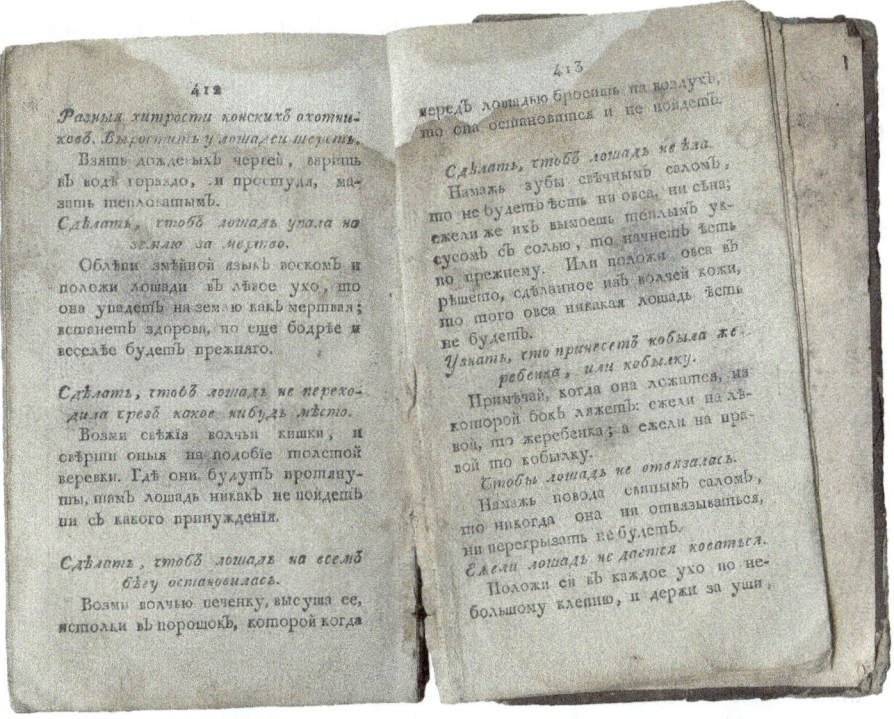

Ill. 12. "Full Town and Village Horse Doctor"

Though we have to remember that we are talking about a time when books were not read but learned by heart.

Such literature first appeared in Russia during the time of Alex Michailovich and then found an audience in the Russian public.

The rare eighteenth century book, "Full Town and Village Horse Doctor" (ill. 12), partially translated into Russian, was an almanac of practical advice with slightly less cruel recipes such as "how to stop a horse without the use of the bridle". The recipe there was simple and clear. Not as dark as the Gothic French one.

41

"Take a wolf's liver, dry it, pound it into a powder. Throwing the powder into the air in front of a horse will stop it." (page 11)

And an amusing way to lay a horse down: "Stick beeswax on a snake's tongue and place it into the horses' left ear —the horse will fall on the ground as if dead".

All of this is very entertaining without doubt, but we must still return to our PRINCEPS QUAESITUM.

XII

It is enough to look at the nerve patterns in a horse's back to understand how sensitive it is. It is no accident of course that the anatomical structure of the horse's nervous system is so extraordinarily well constructed.

It was no accident that the medial branches of the *nervi spinales* (the spinal cord nerves) which come out from the spinal cord (*medulla spinalis*) which is directly connected with the brain were placed so high on a horse's back, under (and into) the very epidermis, above the the spinous processes.

Besides the obvious biomechanical function, the back has another very important function. The spinal cord's work is to guarantee that the responses from the entire nervous system can communicate the senses of taste, smell, vision, hearing, and vestibular function to the brain, not to get lost in too much detail.

On this especially vulnerable, sensitive organ, onto the *medulla spinalis*, the brain of the back, sits a rider.

XIII

It is possible to pull the wool over ones eyes, reassuring a rider that the saddle gullet has the very curve and depth that prevents a rider's influence on the spinal cord.

But this consolation is for idiots. The medial branches of the spinal cord nerve, the primary organ which signals an external problem, are widespread, and are not in any way protected from the pressure of the saddle.

The gullet would need to be widened three to four times in order to minimize the rider's influence on them, which is unrealistic.

Elementary physiology proves the understanding that with the slightest breach of the School SPATIUMS by the rider, this serious pain inflicting factor will not only compromise the muscles of back but the spinal cord as well.

It isn't a conventional way to think that the horse's back is the home of the spinal cord brain and is not made for any external loadings, it has completely different functions.

XIV

A horse's back is not a seat, not a place for a human butt, not a piece of "meat", not some sort of "terra firma". It is a very complex and tender anatomical structure with extraordinary functions.

Without any harm being done, without alarming the nerves or progressing to pain or damage, is it possible for a rider to sit astride a horse's back?

It is!

For the first 10–15 minutes, the back is strong and powerful (if the horse has been properly gymnasticized in hand and at liberty); the muscular system of the back is capable of taking care of itself.

But I repeat, only for a short duration as aforesaid in this "Tractate" in the chapter about Spatiums.

And only under the condition of an absolutely reverent relation of a rider to this back.

Of course with the absence of any metal which would mutilate the horse as well as its movements.

And only under the condition of an absolutely correct School seat, which is not a result of numbly repeated schooling exercises but is the direct consequence of true relations with a horse, of knowledge of a horse, complete absence of fear of it, and full absence of any "adrenalin rush" in a rider.

Frigusculum

XV

It is appropriate to mention one more obligatory factor that is casually mentioned as self-evident in almost every one of the old School essays and is directly addressed in "PRAECEPTIO PRAECEPTORIBUS".

This factor is called FRIGUSCULUM which, translated, means "chill" (ill. 13 a, b).

It addresses the state of a rider's spirit, the complete absence of adrenalin, any impulsiveness, any excitement.

FRIGUSCULUM cannot be considered nonchalant; it is more a light, chilly irony, ideal, a little derisive, chilly indulgence.

This feeling must be shown on the face, and it must define all behavior and override any panic tendencies in the rider.

By the way, during work in hand FRIGUSCULUM is also strictly required. Excitement is as inappropriate as anger.

Ill. 13a. Frigusculum under saddle

Ill. 13b. Frigusculum in hand

The most important psychological instrument prescribed by the School is FRIGUS-CULUM. This feeling must be directed towards the horse and yourself.

This "chill" does not preclude love, gentleness and compassion.

XVI

The use of this instrument is mandatory if there is a desire to teach a horse and achieve a real relationship with her. Especially on a horse's back, when this chilly irony (ironic dispassionateness) must saturate the entire human organism.

I will say honestly that of all the School-approved methods, FRIGUSCULUM is the most amazingly effective and is the most difficult one.

XVII

Lets get back to horseback.

There is, by the way, an obligatory School exercise that forms the "reverentia", a word probably descended from the Latin word meaning awe, reverence, the essence of which is that a teacher during work in hand places his bare hands (or in very thin gloves) on different areas of a horse's back, "listening" to it through the palms and learning the unique rhythm of each horse, grasping the sensitivity of its "breath".

I assure you that half a year of reverent exercises is enough to learn to understand and respect a horse's back. Palms must be placed on the back of a walking, trotting and cantering horse comfortably and tightly.

In the case of a canter it is only allowed to have one palm on the horse's back. The canter must be very collected of course; a change of canter to caracole or terre-a-terre is possible.

This exercise looks difficult at first glance but it is very simple.

With very definite and clever work in hand from the ground, the palms' placement on a horse's back and their hold on it during its movement isn't difficult at all.

Besides this reverent exercise is one of the "permits" needed to gain access to a horse's back. I cannot prescribe the length of holding the palms on the back.

It has been said in school when there are difficulties in learning the works of ancient authors "to continue learning until there is understanding" (ill. 14).

So, there is still some hope, having obeyed all rules of safety, having obeyed every one of the School rules and Spatiums, of course a rider "can".

But "can" does not mean, "must".

And this "can" isn't an acceptable answer to our PRINCEPS QUAESITUM, "Why?"

46

XVIII

Naturally, neither physiologically, nor anatomically, nor psychologically has a single horse EVER desired to have someone sit on its spine and spinal cord brain, to disturb the natural biomechanics of her movements, her natural organic balance, equilibrium and the feeling of freedom.

Ill. 14. Reverentia

XIX

Every time a typical rider climbs onto a horse, it is for her a huge physiological and psychological shock and cannot be a "desired" event because not a single horse has a desire to feel sharp pain in the muscles of the back, loins, neck or in the proximal area of the chest.

XX

To assume that a horse has accepted it or feels "pleasure" from this means to assume that under the skin of a horse hides an absolutely perverted alien, an extraterrestrial type of conscious mind that makes a horse into a creature who does not take into account her physiological sensations or absolutely disregards them.

You understand that this is impossible. Even the slightest misunderstanding of such a delicate question as physiological qualities is a guarantee for the quick extinction of the entire species and is unheard of in nature.

But this isn't something we need to talk about because we see that the reflexive system in horses is the same as in all mammals.

Reaction to pain and discomfort (when there is a way express it) is very quick and strong. Physiological systems determine the animal's psychology and state of mind.

> **But! Both metal and rider are instruments of torture, which cruelly plague the horse and aggressively and destructively affect her physiology. The torture of metal, for instance, is an undeniable scientific fact.**

But they do demonstrate the formal submissiveness of a horse to the "metal-controlled" process of amateur horsemanship*.

XXI

Here we can draw two conclusions. First of all, we get more proof of torture and the absolute power of control through NCS by metal-induced means. But this is already clear and common.

The second conclusion, regardless of its obviousness — is far more important. By analyzing this situation we gain proof of the mental capabilities of a horse.

Horror inspired by a human and his devices, absolute understanding of the futility of rebellion, understanding the consequences of disobedience and that the outcome of what follows is not simply being beaten but the sophisticated tortures of "being taught a lesson".

All of this is likely to be imagined by a horse. And imagined well.

Nothing else can explain the wild contradiction between the physiological factors and formal obedience. If horses weren't so clever, then when they would see bridles,

---

* Any non-School member who rides is viewed as an amateur, regardless of who practices it, Anky van Grunsven or a "mucky girl" hanging out at a metro station.

spurs or sportsmen who are firmly associated in their minds with the concept of torture, they would rebel desperately.

Each and every time.

XXII

It needs to be said that this isn't my own discovery but a belief that is firm and consistent within the School. I have only tailored this belief to today's concepts.

Even in "PRAECEPTIO PRAECEPTORIBUS", the magical and secretive book of the School, much is said about the main mystery of a horse, about her amazing mind and similarity of this mind with a human one.

This is probably the reason why the manuscripts emphatically forbid the School Masters to believe in Christianity.

After digging for some time in "PRAECEPTIO PRAECEPTORIBUS" and other manuscripts, it becomes clear that any anthropocentric religion viciously limits the mind and places a human being into some sort of special category of creatures.

It is amusing at first glance but from the point of view of the School, it is unacceptable and deeply fallacious because it destroys those natural bonds that exist between a man and a horse, which are a great help in her education.

It is hard not to notice that honest rudeness which this seemingly saintly Christian manuscript (the Bible) allows for in relation to a horse:

"Do not be like the horse or the mule, which have no understanding but must be controlled by bit and bridle or they will not come to you (Psalm 32:9) "Be ye not as the horse, nor as the mule, which have no understanding: whose mouth must be held in with bit and bridle, lest they come near unto thee." (Psalm 32:9) "A whip is for the horse, a bridle for the ass, and a rod for the fool's back." (Proverbs 26:3) "Behold, we put bits in the horses' mouths, that they may obey us; and we turn about their whole body" (James 3:3)

And so forth. Besides, it needs to be understood that bits in the bible are first of all a symbol of the humiliation of an enemy, a symbol of punishment and terror.

The god of the bible, when arranging another hysterical and momentous showdown, threatens: "Because thy rage against me and thy tumult is come up into mine ears, therefore I will put my hook in thy nose, and my bridle in thy lips, and I will turn thee back by the way by which thou camest." (2 Kings 19:28)

In the last quote, the threats aren't addressed towards a horse but for a human and in god's tongue they mean the highest level of humiliation and punishment.

XXIII

Besides, I was a little too hash. The inadmissibility of Christianity within the School is based not only on this religion creating problems in the School's work, destroying mystical and biological connections between human and horse.

XXIV

It is not even based on the honestly spiteful rudeness of the "holy manuscript" towards a horse.

XXV

One has to remember the Templar origins of the School, the hidden spiritual allegiance of the School masters to Kabbalah and to many mysterious and wise doctrines, which have always been in conflict with Christianity.

It needs to be remembered that the spiritual ancestors of the School are people from the order of the Temple of Solomon, i.e., Templars — which was destroyed by Christians.

XXVI

Naturally, the ancestors of the spiritual Templar tradition have absolutely no gentle feelings or respect towards this religion and never could have.

Naturally, it cannot be forgotten that through Newcastle as well as through other English School masters who had a powerful formative role in the School ideology, there was also the influence of Rosicrucians and Francis Bacon, who were also hostile to Christianity.

XXVII

It is no accident that the old School emblem that decorates many pages of "PRAECEPTIO PRAECEPTORIBUS" contains Templar, Freemason, Rosicrucian and Kabbalistic symbols but not a single Christian one. The central cross that is crowned by horse and human skulls, entwined by the snake of cognition of good and evil is the Egyptian cross TAU* which has nothing to do with Christianity (ill. 15).

"...Butt devouring..."

XXVIII

Actually the old School manuscripts can be very honest.

---

* In other translations, it is sometimes called the crook of Moses.

Ill. 15. Old Emblem of the School

There are surprising but clear instructions for the need for the vegetarianism of School masters who desire to "perfect the School seat", to be found in paragraph XVI. Here, the rules of "PREACEPTIO PREACEPTORIBUS" are dry, categorical and definite.

You cannot eat meat and that is all.

Only in the additional writings at the end of the book, one of the authors has put forth a very short but genius explanation: "If you can eat horsemeat* from a plate, boiled or smoked, then you will learn also to devour it with your butt, feeding yourself on its movements or having fun, and will never be able to sit properly. Getting on a horse's back you must sit in order to SERVE a horse, not to have fun on it or to devour its power".

XXIX

It needs to be said that regardless of the directness and impudence the School's entire worldview is contained in this phrase. Vegetarianism is first of all a respect for another's life and sufferings; it is the moral impossibility of the use of someone's death or suffering for one's own pleasure or consumption.

Of course, a viewpoint like that about a horse will always be unpopular. In this way the School has never even tried to look like it is "something for the masses" it is an elite discipline. Even to understand where the School ends as a spiritual practice and where it begins as a mastership of the education of a horse is very difficult at times. One is very strongly dependent on the other. None of this is surprising really. There are plebeian ways to be entertained, like equestrian sport, that are based on stupidity, cruelty and a desire to have fun, to excite one's reflexes and instincts.

And there are spiritual practices based on science, mastership, intelligence and a large amount of knowledge.

---

* I have written the quote about horsemeat here, but the book refers to every type of meat, repeatedly and with confidence.

51

Of course these practices cannot be for the masses.

And they mustn't be.

XXX

But I strayed a little from the topic. We were talking about a back. A horse's physiology does not give a verdict about the presence of a human on a horse's back, when strict rules for safety and Spatiums are obeyed, of course.

(But this "feeble" pass is not an answer to our PRINCEPS QUAESITUM in even the smallest way.)

The difficulty of the question requires that we must take a very deep look into it, so lets go on about the back.

XXXI

In learning about a correct relationship to the horse's back neither classical dressage nor sports can help. Actually it is the opposite, they will help one to get into wrong relationships.

A search for even one tiny, microscopic, rational grain of knowledge in the sphere of the "classics" as well as in sports will yield no results. Any ideas about a horse from these disciplines are pure stupidity.

XXXII

As we have already said, in sports as well as in classical riding — NCS (neurocranial shock)* is the main method for influencing a horse. Affecting the nervous system of the head is the purpose for the metal in the mouth. NCS creates a factor that can paralyze the horse by pain. This strictly mechanical influence is responsible for wounding the brain with characteristic damage to the epidural and subdural areas of the brain as well as concussion to the brain itself.

All of these are scientifically proven facts.

---

* For verbal clarification of the actions that are representing the primary techniques that enable the obedience of a horse in ES we use a special term "NEUROCRANIALIS SHOCK (shock of the nerve system of the skull). This term is highly correct and very capacious.

In the use of method (let's call it) N.1, we see a very rigid rein grab by one hand and a very strong pull by the other hand, which is so powerful that half of the bit rushes through the horse's mouth, and the rider's elbow goes back as far as it is possible. This sharp elbow movement increases the leverage force of the bit accordingly, and results in an especially severe and painful blow to the left or right part of horse's skull.

Method N. 2 represents an even sharper direct blow by the bit, over all the sensitive areas of horse's mouth. As a rule, every horse who has been forced this way, tries to weaken the effect of the blow by tossing its head up.

XXXIII

Metal in a horse's mouth can be compared to an electric shock device by its effective impact on the brain.

XXXIV

Show-jumping horses receive 20–30 neurocranial shocks during a single competition (these numbers are averaged).

Dressage horses, due to the tricky influence of the trigimenal nerves, are in neurocranial shock all the time.

XXXV

Even the most superficial look at dressage is enough to notice that all of its normative movements contradict the anatomy of a horse and are in direct conflict with it. Naturally, the state of constant NCS forms a special quality of movements. For the audience of this sport, these spasmodic pain-induced movements have become the standard.

XXXVI

Its funny to watch how a crowd of judges and sportsmen discuss the topic of the "naturalness" of movements, while watching a horse that has a device in her mouth giving her signals similar to electroshock therapy.

XXXVII

(I am very sorry for having to stray from the principal topic of this tractate occasionally to destroy prejudices. Luckily, these prejudices break as easily as rotten nuts and can be done along the way. The public has the same uncivilized and wild approach to a horse's back. In its essence, their approach is a cocktail made from ignorance, stereotypes and stupidity.)

Butt-mania

XXXVIII

One of the principal mistakes that destroys a horse and makes her suffer a great deal is known as "butt-mania". Lets deal with this.

It needs to be remembered that the standard of the so called "naturalness" of a horse's movements was introduced and developed by humans, which is, if you think about it, funny in itself.

What is even more ridiculous is that regardless of the fact that a horse's anatomy does not change, this standard has been revised several times due to changes in fashion, painting, sculpture and the influences of Haute Ecole (HE), riding schools, etc.

XXXIX

But the funniest thing is that those people who developed that standard have never watched horses whose movements are free from pain-induced control.

Moreover, these people seriously assumed that the communication between a horse and rider is impossible without control through pain.

XL

In other words, the standard of horse behavior in sports is the behavior in the moment when a horse suffers severe oral and cranial pain, pain from spurs, serious painful sensations in the lumbosacral areas of the spinal cord, pains in the atlanto-occipital joint, in the salivary glands down behind the ears and the extremely painful myological sensations stemming from the rider's weight, bringing about hysterical arousal, caused by pain and leading to a feeling of complete desperation, due to the "impossibility of changing an unbearable situation".

XLI

Naturally, the sum of these physiological and psychological sufferings has dictated the painful quality of the movements and style of behavior.

And this has BECOME THE NORM, in sport, as well as in painting, sculpture, photography and literature.

XLII

This is the brief horrific and insane history of dressage.

XLIII

This is the same as if the standard of natural human behavior would be a human's behavior on an electric chair.

54

The writhing, convulsions, dripping saliva, uncontrollable defecation — if all this were considered the standard of grace and good manners, a standard to live up to, then anyone who acts differently could be accused of unnatural behavior, of being shy and having bad manners.

Yes, the movements of a human on an electric chair would probably look very entertaining yet very different than what they would be in a normal chair.

It is the same with horse, her true agility when free from painful influence would be very different than what is normal in sport, on engravings and in sculptures (ill. 16).

XLIV

The problem with every "expert", of every judge of a horse's grace is that they HAVEN'T THE SLIGHTEST CLUE of how a horse moves when there is no pain-induced control.

The biomechanics of a truly natural, healthy horse are absolutely unknown to them. They have no point of reference.

They are used to comparing between different painful versions and to have only painful variations of movements as a reference point.

XLV

All of this is very sad, but oh well, this is how it is.

The cornerstone of their perceptions of movements may be called butt-mania (the maniacal belief that the caudal area is the "engine" of a horse).

A standard practice is the forceful pain of "driving the haunches" at all costs.

What is interesting, this "engagement of the hindquarters" doesn't mobilize many of those powerful layers of caudal area muscles on which the bet is being placed.

Only external coherence with a farfetched classical picture is being created, but actually the colossal caudal muscles stay cheerlessly "quiet" — *m. biceps femoris* and *m. gluteus medius*, and what is the most surprising, even the "sweet couple" — *m. semitendinosus* and *m. semimembraosus*, form a huge caudal "cone" of muscles which are quite active in normal horse movements, yet in typical dressage, they are silent.

I have purposefully named only those muscles whose work is visible to the eye.

Actually, any kind of mobilization, and especially a strong one in the caudal area, when extreme myological functions are performed, must show a visible, absolutely clear tensioning of the "big cone" of muscles, as shown when a horse performs the pesade.

Ill. 16. School exercise for the development of MAGNITUDO

But this doesn't happen during a forced (with the help of bit and spur) push of the hindquarters.

The muscles are morosely quiet. During strenuous activity, with a horse using her muscles at 70–80 percent of their capacity, we see only the tensioning of the tensor fasciae latae (and very moderately) the superficial gluteal muscle.

XLVI

This anatomical mystery is very easily solved. A horse is an exact science.

When forcefully contracting a horse by traditional techniques (bit+spur) the rider painfully influences every central branch of every nerve of the lumbosacral plexus.

All these nerves, strictly speaking, serve the powerful ischiatic nerve, and are absolutely indifferent to the beauties and standards of classical dressage; they are absolutely indifferent to pirouettes, and passages.

Their business is to innervate the muscles so that the spinal cord stays unharmed. Remember that through whatever muscles they go, wherever they branch laterally or dorsally, whatever they innervate "along the way" — they were, are and will always be loyal servants of the spinal cord.

And during a strong activation of the "big cone" of muscles, naturally, with "hindquarters engaged", will have a "bending" influence on the lumbar area of the spine, creating additional danger for the medulla spinalis.

That is why they are keeping themselves "quiet", not playing the game, not engaging the colossal caudals!

XLVII

In short, everything would have been great and the classical scheme would have been blameless and effective if it were created exclusively from a horse's head and hindquarters and in between there was no back or loin, which are the keepers of the medulla spinalis, the spinal cord.

XLVIII

To formulate it briefly and without literacy: during the moment of a forceful push of the hind legs, the spinal cord nerves turn off the most powerful muscles of the hindquarters in order to avoid a bend in the spinal cord between the fused sacrum and the slightly flexible lumbar vertebrae in order to save the spinal cord from injuries.

What this means is that these "butt-mania" people are achieving the opposite of what they desire. And the more they push the hindquarters, the weaker they become.

57

XLIX

Naturally, by means of metal influence in the mouth and of spurs, the caudal muscles can be mobilized but with an obligatory deformation of the spinal cord and its brain.

Of course, everything said above does not preclude a short and very light push of the hind legs under the body but this push has to be phased, its degree can only be judged by the horse itself and no one else to avoid damage to the spinal cord and movement.

A person is not allowed to interfere with this process.

L

It needs to be remembered that one fallacy, the most ridiculous one, exists — the fallacy that it is possible to make the spinal cord more flexible.

I am telling you that to develop spinal cord flexibility, i.e., to make the microscopic gaps between vertebras (corpus vertebrae) bigger can be done only surgically, and in no other way.

LI

If we look carefully at a free and light but slightly collected cantering horse (table A), who was given the right to determine the amount of collection and mobilization of the hindquarter muscles, a horse free from the effects of "metal" and "heel", then we will see a myological picture that is live and natural.

LII

If we look with enough attention at this illustration (ill. 17), then we can understand the insignificant extent that movements of a rider's body will have to cause a lift and bigger hind leg drive under the body.

These slight movements of body are the maximum that a rider can allow himself, any other means of influence are a misdirected attempt to affect biomechanics and anatomy and therefore, will get you the opposite result and will produce traumas to the entire lumbosacral area.

LIII

Any attempt to use spur is proof of stupidity and ignorance.

Ill. 17. A slight movement of the rider's body provokes the lift of the hind legs and their placement deeper under the horse's body.

MAGNITUDO
Gallop

Wounds from spurs on the horse's sides and stomach are what typically reveal the "mercilessness" of a spur.

This, however, is the most innocent out of all consequences of its use.

Spurs leave a bigger trauma in a different place, provoking those processes that the "myological mind" is trying to avoid at all costs, the spinal cord brain suffers from it too.

Spurs on a rider's heels are a sign of the human's low level of understanding about what he wants and how it is achieved.

LIV

Actually, the history of "butt-mania" is a long and interesting one. Butt psychosis derived in sport from classical dressage and for some reason the idea lodged in peoples' heads.

Where did it all begin? Somewhere Xenophon mentioned the need of the hindquarters to push.

It was casually mentioned, due to him not knowing exactly how it could be achieved. It was suggested that the best way is to push the hinds with help of assistants, who whip the horse's hindquarters from both sides. Early School masters — Fiaschi and Grizone — were greedily looking for a theoretical base, in Xenophon they found a thought and grabbed on to it with all their immoderate Neapolitan passion in their worship of him. And everything was put straight into practice! "Hand spurs" were invented with "claws" and "knobs", which were held in the rider's armpits, hooks with reins were pierced into the skin of the hindquarters and a rider would pull them on every stride to "push the hindquarters under the horse". Fiaschi, as it is well known, would break a horse with screaming and scratching cats tied to sticks which were then directed at the horse's hips, Kavendish had been tying hedgehogs to his horses' tails (in another version to a blanket on the hindquarters) and to the inside of the thighs (into the skin) hand bells were attached, etc, etc.

For a short time "butt-mania" fell silent, Pluvinel derisively smashed it, but after his death everything began again with a new face.

Today we are seeing the resurgence of this "butt psychosis".

There are too many followers of the "butt-mania" school to count; it's easier to say who hasn't been one. Especially enraged ones were de Klamm, Abzak (Pier-Marie*), Antoine d'Aure, adepts of the school of Berenger, the school of Eizenberg, Decarpentri and, of course, of Boshe and Fillis (illustration with gravures from the book).

So, there are enough illustrations it seems.

---

* There were many Abzaks, the School history knows of three: Pier-Marie (1744–1827), Jan-Fransua (1747–1831), Alexis (precise years of life are unknown).

61

LV

We are left only with the answer to the main question, to our PRINCEPS QUAESITUM.

One of the mysterious unnamed authors of "PRAECEPTIO PRAECEPTORIBUS" has answered it astonishingly by writing that a rider ought to "serve" a horse while being astride. Honestly, this is very exalted for me, overly literate and because of that, leaves it open to interpretation.

(To confess, this mystery and grandiloquence of "PRAECEPTIO PRAECEPTORIBUS" sometimes drives me mad.)

LVI

The essence of the answer is simple — a rider can get on a horse's back only in order to prove to a horse that a human isn't scary and isn't dangerous in any way by his mastery and gentleness, not from the ground or from above.

Naturally, this evidence can only be given to a horse when you have it and know how. It can only be done if you are absolutely ready to give the horse a piece of your own knowledge by making her healthier, stronger and wiser.

In short, using the language of the old manuscripts, if you are ready to "serve a horse".

THE SCHOOL SEAT

Chapter Four

I

When a man appears on the back of a horse, he takes some sort of a position, and this position has its own features.

This position is called a "seat".

It is believed that there are many different types of "seats". Special seats for show-jumping, for trail riding, for bullfighting and so on and so forth.

To put it simply, that's not true.

There are not many different types of seats; there are a great number of perversions on the topic of "seat".

We won't look at them, there are too many of them, and unfortunately all of them are factors that lead to "uncomfortable and then painful sensations" for the horse.

If you put any man on a horse without a saddle, you will always get approximately the same seat. It can vary a bit due to some anatomical peculiarities of the individual man or horse, but its principle will stay the same.

It will be a very deep seat with absolutely relaxed leg, with the toes pulled down and out a bit with fixed thighs.

This seat will appear without any effort on the person's part. The back of the horse itself, its form, the construction of the whole horse, will distribute a man's body exactly like this, no other way (ill. 18).

II

This will be the most natural seat.

This will be the rider's position on a horse, which is naturally dictated by the features of the horse's body, a man's body and the necessity of a man to sit in comfortable balance on the horse.

Surprisingly, if we look at old engravings in the works of Pluvinel, Gaspar Sonie, Dupatie du Clamme, closely enough we'll see an illustration of this seat. (ill. 19).

Ill. 18. True "School Seat"

Can you recognize it? This is the very "School seat" by its classical description. This is how a "school seat" was pictured in folios of the XVII-XVIII centuries, in the works of School masters. Although the riders in old engravings sit on saddles, they sit as if there are no saddles and they just take the natural position, which is taken by a man

65

on a horse's bare back. Moreover, Antoine de Pluvinel in his work gave a complete written description, especially bringing attention to the position of the thigh. However, we'll return to the thighs a bit later. A School seat is possible either with a saddle or without it. Naturally, with very strong movements of a horse, the rider will re-

Ill. 19. Old engravings showing the "School Seat"

spond by a light lifting of the knees and decline of the body angle, but the principle of "deepness" and naturalness won't disappear.

So, let's sum up the features, signs and attendant circumstances of the School seat.

1. Spatium

III

"Spatium" is an old School name for the time during which a rider can be on horseback.

Our spatium equals 15 minutes. Why?

Because our primary target is not to cause discomfort and pain in the muscles and skin of a horse's back.

66

That is why the maximum "School" period of being on horseback is exactly 15 minutes. Notably, I stress, that is the utmost maximum.

After 15 minutes under the weight and pressure of rider and saddle, the microtrauma of tissues begin, the compression effect accumulates, and the back of the horse begins to feel light discomfort. Dermal receptors produce an "itchy"* feeling. Under the impact of direct compression, under the weight of the rider and saddle, the "perimysium", the sheath of connective tissue surrounding muscle fibers, begins primary deformation, accompanied by feelings of discomfort, then these symptoms become more acute. At the end of 20 minutes, they turn into the feeling of dull pain (ill. 20).

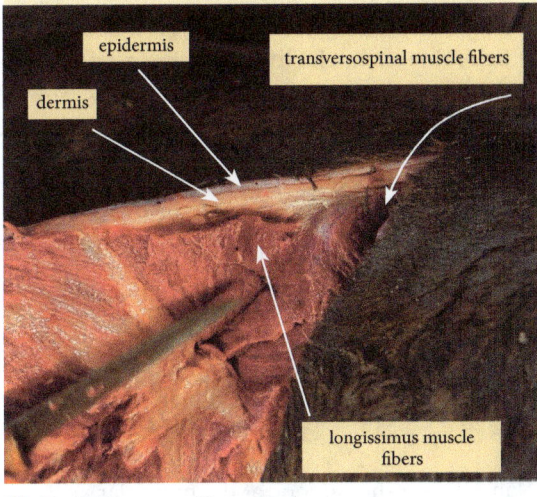

Dissection #75 (anatomic region — *perimysium, fasciculus muscularis*) "Compression effect", tissue deformation after 15 minutes of horseback riding

epidermis

transversospinal muscle fibers

dermis

longissimus muscle fibers

Ill. 20. © Nevzorov Haute Ecole

These figures were determined through research and experiments on the soft back tissues, muscle fascicles, fasciculus muscularis, perimysium, endomysium and epimysium.

Direct pressure of the weight (rider + a tightened saddle) — in the first 12–15 minutes didn't cause any tissue deformation.

(Which means that it doesn't cause negative feelings stemming from physiology.)

After 12–15 minutes the "compression effect" began, myofibrils and perimysium began "yielding to" the pressure, which in terms of physiology translates to "the onset of physiological feelings of discomfort".

Why does this happen?

IV

The issue at hand is that every muscle contains a microvascular system of blood and lymph venules and capillaries that create within a muscle (roughly speaking) its own

---

* An itching sensation appears a bit earlier than myological discomfort, but in the first stage it is practically unnoticeable..

67

microcirculation. Compression breaks it down, nourishment of the *fasciculus muscularis* reduces or stops — and the "compromised" muscle sounds the alarm through branches of nerve fibers.

There is no tragedy yet, no pain yet, neither perimysium nor fasciclulus are damaged, but the muscle is already disgusted. This indignation does not "shout" yet, it is in "grumbling" mode.

But this grumbling is already clear, already conscious.

So we must understand that even with an ideally fitted saddle and an ideal School seat, a strict limit of being astride is 12–15 minutes. (*Editor's note:* Later this time was shortened to five minutes. Now Nevzorov has fully rejected horseback riding).

That's the science of it.

In addition, I wouldn't be as generous as science allows and for different horses I would require different spatiums.

For horses from four to five years old — the spatium is five minutes.

From ages five to six — 10 minutes.

From six until death — 12–15 minutes.

V

Naturally we should look at the muscular anatomy of each individual horse.

There is an ideal, athletically developed musculature, developed during work "from the ground", "in hand", and "at liberty".

This musculature is developed by consistent work with a horse over a period of two years with exercises such as crunch, shapp, sentado, pesade, Spanish walk in hand, sokel (pedestal), games and so on.

But what happens, of course, is that there is often a partial or complete dystrophy of the muscles, especially in horses that have been used for equestrian sport the trapezius muscle is in a state of dystrophy. In this case, bravely shorten the spatium in half until the muscles are recovered.

So:

Any effects of a man on horseback can be classified in the following way according to simple physiology:

One to 15 minutes: lack of specific sensations.

Fifteen to 30 minutes: increasing sensations until discomfort is reached.

68

Everything that is over 30 minutes can be characterized by simple physiological analysis as "strong pain".
Everything that follows induces trauma.

Thermograms validate simple and indisputable physiological facts, they show the degree of chronic or acute effects on both myological and locomotive apparatuses.

Healthy sport or riding horses just DON'T EXIST. If there are, then they exist only in the FMG (folklore of mucky girls).

VI

Here we won't discuss exactly what makes a horse bear pain in his back resulting from hour-long training or due to trail rides so beloved by bumpkins.

Everything is known. An article "Dressage, Let's Dot the Is and Cross the T's" has dotted the i's in this question.

There isn't a single living creature that goes through painful torture of such strength and length as a horse in so-called "equestrian sport".

A horse's problem, however strange it may sound, is in his intellect and fantastic mind.

VII

Imagine that YOUR WHOLE LIFE consisted of only painful feelings of differing degrees of strength and duration.

The first, the second and the third kinds of pain are the brightest events of each day. You know only three realities.

Waiting for pain. Memories about pain. The feeling of pain.

These three realities are the only content of a horse's life. There is practically nothing more in the life of a horse who is in man's grasp. Pain forms the world-view and behavior patterns, pain determines and denotes even the times of day.

A horse begins to feel the necessity of fitting in and somehow easing her pain by degrees. A horse makes choices, understanding that itching, a simple dull pain, is more preferable than acute and paralyzing pain (in its mouth).

Prostrating to the one who causes pain — this is from the same paradigm.

VIII

Stories of sportsmen about horses who take bits into their mouth by themselves sound incredibly funny.

69

Does history not have enough examples of people who, when committed to execution dug graves for themselves BY THEMSELVES?

Yes, they knew about the execution, about a bullet to the back of the head an hour later, about the fact that THEY will lie and decay in the hole they are digging. But fear of terrible beatings, of being cut with shovels, of crushing blows by iron, made them DIG.

During "pleasure riding" which is so beloved by "mucky girls", the horse with his perfect mind is moved by a terrible fear of a stronger torture than a one-time torture by the bit or pain in a numb and itching back.

Every horse once refused to take a bit. And he remembers clearly the hell he had to go through because of this "refusing".

His brilliant memory holds onto everything with all the nuances, with all emotional accents, with all his personal marks.

The better you understand it, the easier it is for you to educate the horse. The less you "stupidize" a horse in your mind, the closer you come to the real situation of things. Let's leave to "mucky girls" one of the most stupid statements about the necessity of rewarding a horse directly AFTER an achievement (an example of "stupidizing").

Truly, a sportsman's treatment of a horse is as a mysterious, indistinct, huge piece of meat with a momentary memory.

But all this is just lyrical digression… I suggest we come back to the topic of our Tractate on a School Mount.

2. Interdictum

IX

Now we are passing on to "interdiction" i.e. to what is inadmissible and what categorically contradicts the principles of the School seat.

Asking for apologies from the reader, but for headings of this part of the tractate I took the very old School terms for absolutely selfish reasons. I feel comfortable with them, as I hope they will become for everyone who wants to understand the essence and features of the School seat.

So, the absolutely inadmissible things are the "posting trot" and absolutely everything that is connected with putting weight in the stirrups as well as gripping with the thighs, or "working the loins", i.e. an awful rubbing against a saddle with ones genitals.

70

It seems that the interdiction of these two ridiculous perversions don't need any comments, but I will briefly clarify some things.

Both varieties of distortions are impossible (or extremely uncomfortable) with a natural seat on a bare horse's back, and this by itself moves them to the list of artificial gimmicks interdicted by the School.

X

The so-called "posting trot" is the hardest and the most dangerous for horse (ill. 21).

The assumption that a rider's weight eases in some magical way, by means of rising above horses' back, resting against stirrups, is of course, a load of rubbish.

The rider's weight stays with him. It doesn't disappear anywhere.

The pressure on the horse's back only increases through the amplitude of body movements up and down, which I hope is all that needs to be said.

Moreover, every push on the stirrups during the rising of a rider's body, multiplies the rider's weight by 10–12 percent.

This leads to more forceful pressure on a smaller area of the saddle on the horse's back. This pressure is always uncomfortable and painful for soft back tissues.

Stand on a scale again but this time on the floor, and try to crouch and stand up with force as if you're posting the trot.

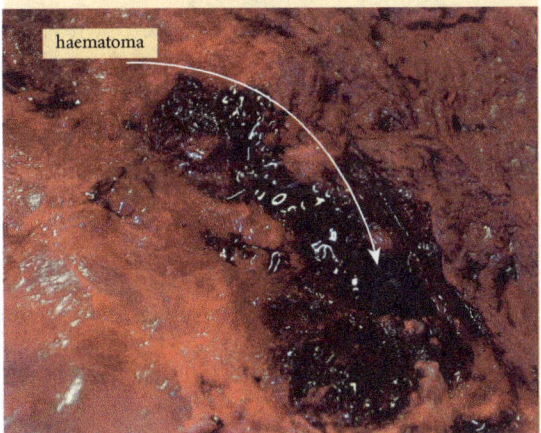

Dissection #250 (anatomic region — *haematoma hipodermaticum*) Haematoma of the back's soft tissues, a typical result of the so-called "posting trot"

haematoma

Ill. 21. © Nevzorov Haute Ecole

You'll see how the scale will go crazy, you'll see unbelievable figures. Live horses' backs during the "posting trot" feel approximately the same as the scale does.

Sudden, strong impacts are passed through the stirrup leathers to the fork of the saddle tree, where the stirrup bars are and right where the saddle panel area is minimal and the stuffing is harder and compresses the most quickly.

71

The back panels, which are the widest and the softest and have an absorbing force, during the rising portion of posting are completely unweighted.

I suppose there is no need for further comment on this question.

> **Let's leave "posting trot" to those barbarians and perverts who are doing "pleasure riding" or so-called "equestrian sport" and whom we must not let close to a horse.**

The so-called "gripping of the thighs", or "working of the loins" is interdicted in the School too. Antoine de Pluvinel wrote that the thighs should be "straight and unmoving".

Besides, there is no "work of the loins".

There are some funny, absolutely obscene, shagging movements, which in fact is the work of genitals.

A horse moves upwards and forward. A rider moves upwards, forwards, and backwards.

A rider, who is astride and who makes funny twists around the saddle, has to return to the starting position.

This return is insensible to both a horse and the laws of physics.

Besides being in guaranteed dissonance with the rhythm of the horse, what is demonstrated by all ladies (of both sexes) doing dressage — five to six shagging movements will surely contribute to an uneven distribution of weight to the front part of the saddle.

The horse's back feels approximately the same problems as during the "posting trot".

These things are so obvious that I'm even hesitating to clarify them.

A true School seat means maximum immobility of a rider in a saddle. It means maximum stability, which has nothing to do with any fussiness and gimmicks, or any consideration to ease ONESELF from discomfort caused by horses' movements (ill. 22a–d).

However, during the true School seat there is no such thing as discomfort.

If a horse was correctly gymnasticized, if there is a true "relationship" between a rider and a horse, if a rider sits in a natural way, which means in the School way, if SPATIUM is strictly observed, then, very likely no discomfort will exist.

Ill. 22 a. A "secure" School seat during the pirouette →

72

Ill. 22 b. School seat in the passage

Ill. 22 c. School seat in the extended canter

Ill. 22 d. School seat during the pesade with rider's body perpendicular to the horse's back →

Of course, all these things are possible only without painful paralyzers in a horse's mouth, such as a bit or tools for painful direction of a horse's head, such as side-pull, bosal, rope halter etc…

3. Magnitudo

XI

Now that we've finished our section about equestrian sport, we can start the substantial part of this chapter of the tractate about the School mount.

The next important condition of the School mount is MAGNITUDO, which means the power of the horse who is correctly prepared for the rider's weight with the help of special exercises.

In order to explain everything exactly and in detail, I'm returning to the thermograms for a moment.

Strictly speaking, thermography isn't an exact diagnostic device.

Locating the presence of inflammation, the thermograph only determines the fact that there is a problem, but doesn't recognize its name.

The more complicated examinations such as ultrasonography, scintillation scanning, x-ray, etc. explore what the thermograms show, and will determine the problem accurately; they will mark and name it.

Nevertheless, the thermograph can still be extremely accurate when it states the health, soundness of muscles, epidermis, joints, and when it identifies the state called the "blue back".

The "blue back" is the first and the most important condition of the School mount and that is the direct offshoot of MAGNITUDO — the correctly developed, absolute power of the horse.

XII

MAGNITUDO has a natural enemy, a mortal and pitiless one… it is so-called "training".

Training is a system that cripples the horse while preparing it for competitions.

All ratios of the so-called training of all the disciplines of the equestrian sport and other ignorant forms of horse usage, sadly, are created in such a way that the horse has no chance.

Forcibly training for long periods will produce movements contradicting the horse's natural biomechanics. Training breaks and hurts his mycological system, destroys joints and destroys his mental state.

What is "training" and what's the difference between training and the School term "MAGNITUDO".

MAGNITUDO is a very honorable desire to give a horse the full value of his myological condition, to exercise him, to develop his muscles just how they were designed by nature to work.

XIII

Training is an aspiration to adapt the horses' myology to the sport standards, which is based on the painful distortion of natural biomechanics and mind.

> **Even a superficial glance at the movements of the horse gives an opportunity to understand that when performing sports, or the so-called dressage elements, the horse uses completely different muscles than while performing the same element (or very much similar one) at liberty (in games) or in School studies.**

XIV

A simple example; the state of the neck of so-called sport horse.

Every "dressage" horse has a hypertrophic atlas muscle — a muscle that has the function of protection of the atlo-occipital joint from the causes of false collection (forced collection with the bit and restraint of the head).

Broadly speaking, the atlas muscle is the main muscle of the group of "safety muscles"; a guard-muscle, which covers the most vulnerable point of the cervical part. In nature, it has a very average devolvement because it is not used that often.

Any kind of bit hypertrophies it, by reason of its use and the resulting overuse of the muscle. Hypertrophy of the atlas muscle leads to the thinning and necrosis of the splenius, trapezius and serratus muscles, and sets off the whole "opposition muscles" group, which is the sternomandibularis, sternohyoideus and omohyoideus muscles.

This group of muscles works to oppose the rider's hands and the impact of the bit.

No horse manages to escape from the painful action of the bit with the help of this "opposition group". It is this group, which "switches on" with the actions of the hands and iron instruments in the mouth.

(I just can't imagine what kind of fool somebody would be to mix up a horse who was been trained with the bit, with a horse who has been educated without any instruments of enforcement.

77

The muscular presentations of the cervical part are so different, that once you understand this, only a blind man, idiot or sportsman could not see the differences.)

XV

Naturally, the reconstruction of the cervical part, caused by the influence of pain and the bit, spreads a kind of a myological "echo" all over the horse's body.

Practically everything is corrupted... everything, even up to the natural sequence of the muscles' actions; semitendinosus — biceps — gluteal profundus. We can see that in the horse performing passage at liberty or without instruments of enforcement. (table B).

XVI

A sport horse or a horse who has suffered from sports training has an absolutely different sequence of actions that is also easy to see; gluteal profundus — semitendinosus — biceps.

The whole body of the horse falls under a distorted presentation of natural biomechanics, which in fact, leads to the destruction of natural movements and changes them to painful puppet-like ones. Incidentally, suggesting that all the changes of natural biomechanics come only from the painful "echo" of the bit and as a result of the reconstruction of the cervical part would be incorrect, there has not been enough research done about it.

We see an evident destruction of natural biomechanics, it's an unquestionable fact, but maybe the bit is not the only thing that affects it. Perhaps also different kinds of myopathies are connected to the influence of the rider's weight or other "training" features.

XVII

Another question is that when we deal with sportsmen, we deal with an enormous level of cretinism!

Honestly, I'm writing through tears of laughter!

There is such a funny and very exact science to anatomy and its section — myology. All the movements have their anatomical formulas, everything is certain, everything is described and written down by the anatomists who "took a horses' body down to molecules" a long time ago. Notably, such torches like Borelli (ill. 23) began doing it on orders of the old School masters.

XVIII

For example. We need to teach the horse to do an important part of collection — to do a vertical flexion, directing a burst of power from the poll through the nuchal ligament

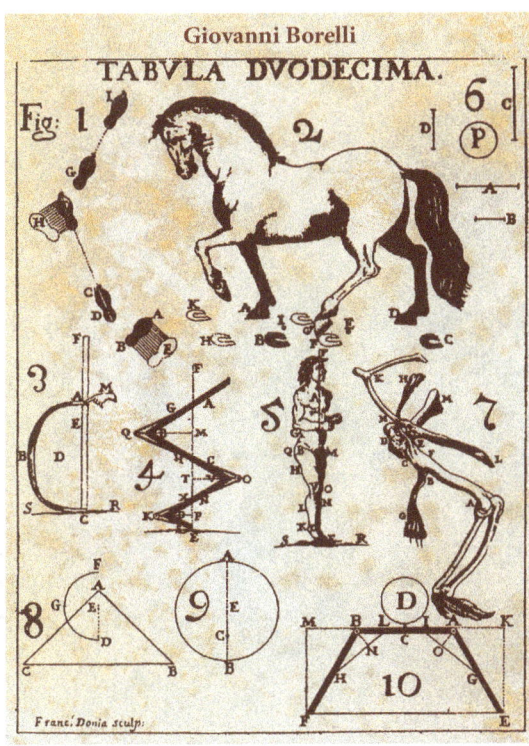

Ill. 23. Myological formula by Borelli

to the latissimus muscle… and a concentrating burst of power from the caudal part… forward, also to the region of m. latissimus dorsi.

Everything is as simple as a kilo of carrots!

Everything is that incredibly simple.

You immediately get a proper, although at first, a rather "hard" collection (due to the special studiousness and dedication of the horse that performs it). That, without a millimeter of strap of course.

XIX

And what does the sportsman do?

He, wishing to teach the horse how to collect, begins exercising the muscles that oppose collection. The muscles of the cervical section that protect the fragile atlo-occipital and atlo-axidalis joints (art. Atlantooccipitalis, art. Atlantoaxidalis) from destruction.

Moreover, this is where the chain reaction starts, due to an unusual anatomic formula, after the atlas muscle is acting, all the muscles of the "opposition" muscles group with the rebellious brachiocephalicus at the head will begin hypertrophying.

Why do they not understand this?!

On the photos (Ill. 24a–b) it can be very well seen how this stupidity is created with the help of the straps and what result they have.

In the table showing passage, I name the myological formulas of natural movements and natural collection.

XX

I exemplified such simple examples so as not to pad the article with straight science. However, for those who want to understand, it is enough.

79

tab. B

MAGNITUDO
Passage

Ill. 24a. Hypertrophy of "opposition-muscles", specific to equestrian sport. The sternohyoid and sternothyroid muscles are hypertrophied. So are the brachiocephalic and atlas muscles; the splenius muscle is atrophied. This is typical of horses used in show-jumping. © G. Gavrilenko

Ill. 24b. It is easy to see how the "opposition-muscles" group, in response to continual pain, has completely depressed the nuchal ligament and unbalanced the ENTIRE myological system of the horse (this is a typical result of equestrian sport). © G. Gavrilenko

This is elementary knowledge, the easiest of all, and even then they try to demonstrate and prove that movements of the horses in equestrian sport are "similar" to the natural movements of the horse, when in fact they have nothing in common.

Myology is as pitiless as physiology, and categorical as well. The breach, the worst breach, of natural myological presentation is that it first provokes a trauma, and then cruelly redoubles it.

In the same way, the so-called training is pathological for any building of the horse-rider relationship. The prominent purpose of training in this context is so-called contact.

Please, name at least one of the world's languages where the words "slave obedience" and "contact" are synonyms?

You won't find it anywhere. Only in the equestrian sports slang.

If they have complete slave obedience, they call it contact. If the horse makes the tiniest attempt to escape from the pain, from the sufferings or rebel against the torture which lasts for too long, or to express somehow his feelings, that means that there is no contact there. And that means that they should achieve contact (slave obedience) with the help of increasing the pain level. That is the simple formula of equestrian sport. And so-called training develops this. (Obnoxiously, everywhere there is only hierachy, lies and vagueness. Simple vagueness that prevents calling obedience, obedience — a beating, a beating and crippling, crippling...

No... They made up their own vocabulary... contact... punishment... training... (Ugh!)

XXI

For the final understanding of the differences between so-called training and MAGNITUDO you should know the following:

1. For the final understanding of the differences between so-called training and MAGNITUDO you should know the following:

2. "Training" serves only itself, not the organism of the horse.

3. "Training" lives off the horse's blood and has an excellent appetite.

4. There is a requirement for "training" if the owner prepares his horse to be eaten. (It's not a coincidence that the rascal-cook* who wished to fry the horses in the hippodromes — and only the blooded horses who had already raced. Right,

---

* Editorial comment: By the "rascal-cook" the author probably means Gordon Ramsay, the horsekiller-cook, England's prophet of horseflesh as an acceptable meat on the dining table.

he knew that racing training incredibly increases the concentration of glycogen in muscle fibres, and that is probably what gives a very special taste to the horse's flesh.)

5. In 99 percent of all the cases, the training is done by only a small "economical factor". "Mucky girls" in the stables, calling themselves riding masters and coaches, make up a new way of earning money, scaring the owners who depend on them, declaring dogmatically that the training is needed for their horse, and in fact, all they do is just cripple him.

By the way, correct myological development can't be given in shocking doses (one or two hours of torture a day).

It is just bottomless stupidity.

XXII

MAGNITUDO, the School's myological preparation of the horse, uses many elements.

Eighty-five percent of these elements and exercises are taught and realized at "liberty" and "from the ground", that means that their descriptions would be more appropriate in the "Tractate on the School Work from the Ground" and not here.

4. Sella

XXIII

A saddle may be considered an accessory as any kind of School work and the most difficult elements are possible without it (Ill. 25).

However, until a horse has a properly muscled state of the back, the saddle is practically an indispensable thing.

Of course you should avoid any sorts of military-derived saddles — Western (Cowboy's), Mongolian or Russian.

It doesn't matter what they call these types of saddles and how much velvet and quilted leather or how many embellishments there are.

"Portuguese" saddles as well as Spanish ones are also of this type. This type of saddle inherently can't be fitted in complete accordance with the asymmetry, nuances and all other singularities of the back of a living horse.

Talk that a saddle of this style is better for a horse's back and has a bigger contact area is again FMG.

I repeat once again, any of these saddles can't be made in precise accordance with measurements of living horses' backs because of their construction and are therefore inadmissible.

83

Saddles of English type are preferable, because of their construction; it is possible to modify them in accordance with the precise measurements of a living horse.

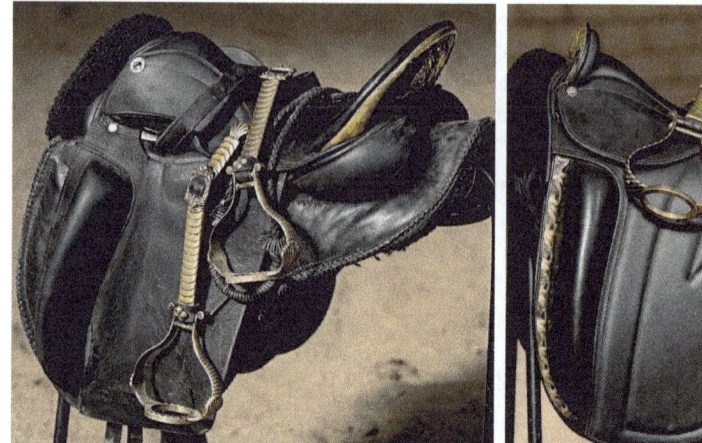

Ill. 25. Ordinary School saddle (left). Ceremonial School saddle (right). © Nevzorov Haute Ecole

However, regardless of saddle type, there is the SPATIUM with its 15 minutes astride and strict limits of manege schooling, strictly controlled work, when it is possible to minimize all feelings of pain and discomfort and to make the effects of a man on horseback practically harmless for the horse herself.

5. Cordeo

XXIV

The School only allows for one auxiliary piece of equipment and that is the CORD-EO — a belt or rope tightly sewn into a ring. I have said a lot about it in the film "Nevzorov Haute Ecole Principles".

In particular, that it must only be used in the area of sixth-seventh neck vertebra, above the prescapularis part of the deep chest muscle or, so to clarify it even further — in the area of the middle part of serratus ventralis muscle of the neck.

At the same time we have to remember that the CORDEO is not and cannot be a means of controlling or restraining a horse.

It is absolutely useless as a pain-inflicting factor in an extreme situation because it can't be a pain inflicting or restraining factor at any time.

If the CORDEO rises higher than the fourth vertebra, it destroys collection and deprives the work with a horse of absolutely any meaning.

Fortunately, a rise to even the second neck vertebra will not produce any impression on a horse at all. The rings of the trachea are a powerful enough structure by themselves, and even at that location the rings are protected from any external trauma by sternohyoid, omohyoid muscles and m. longus capitis.

XXV

Now that self-made imitators of the School have appeared, in the photo 26 a we can notice the typically primitive and ridiculous way the cordeo is being used. There is no relationship with a horse here. A human is trying to turn the cordeo into a means of control, affecting the rings of the trachea, without knowledge that in this position they are absolutely invulnerable and that the "lassoing" of a horse is based on a completely different principle, which is inapplicable in any situation with a cordeo.

XXVI

We are influenced by cartoons, stupid books and absolute lack of anatomical knowledge of the horse and its biomechanics here. (Experiments similar to these were set up by French officers who were lifting the cordeo high, depriving the work of any meaning, and were bringing horses to a state of rebellion due to their inability to get the horse to accomplish any element of dressage. According to testimonies of contemporaries, the picture was disgraceful, pitiful and it all ended in bad way.)

XXVII

By the way, as I've already said, true lassoing technique is based on a completely different principle than the cordeo. It would be good to familiarize oneself with an interesting work by V.K. Darj — «Horse Lassoing as a Traditional Practice of Tuvin-nomads». The principle of the influence of a lasso is that after it has settled on the neck, the rider gallops on his own horse by the side and in front of the horse that has been caught. The lasso is then moved behind the hind legs of the caught horse, which, after the lasso has been tightened falls on its side. The principle used for catching from the ground is about the same. A correctly lassoed horse falls down over its head.

I have given this savage evidence only in order to illustrate the absolute inability of a CORDEO (which doesn't have leverage or a self-tightening loop) as a mean of control or restriction.

Ill. 26a–b. «Kolkhoz», ignorant cordeo use (top) and correct cordeo placement. © A. Davidova, G. Gavrilenko

XXVIII

The use of a CORDEO, if one is serious, is only needed for doing positional corrections and for maintaining straightness in a horse during rearing movements.

It doesn't matter to me at all, what is thought or spoken about the School practice of riding with a cordeo. In this case I'm simply trying to explain that no cordeo can replace the relationship with a horse and with the absence of relationship, will simply become a toy deprived of any power.

In the photo (ill. 26 b) is the correct, School placement of the cordeo.

6. Manege

XXIX

Every School lesson in hand as well as astride must ONLY be accomplished in a manege (ill. 27).

This is a historical tradition and a rule straight from the School, therefore is not open to discussion.

> **The word "Manege", by the way is a pure School word and literally means — "the place for the work… in hand" (it comes from Latin *manus* — hand).**

Regardless of this "undiscussability", and taking into account the unavailability of the fundamental works of the School for a reader, I will shine a light on a few things.

The amount of attention and concentration required from a horse during the learning of practically any Haute Ecole element is as difficult as manually hacking into a secured computer system, or for a Kabbalist decoding the writings of Moshe Ben Shema, or for a professional writing fine literature.

(I cannot recall a single piece of world-class literature written in a tram.)

XXX

To take a horse outside of the attention-centering walls and arcs, the special learning atmosphere of a manege, from the magical smell and collection of sounds— is to seriously interfere with her ability to learn, provoking her absent-mindedness, foolishness or hot-temper.

Yes, it is possible that she will be very obedient outside. And it is possible that it may be even very sustained.

But obedience outside (in a park, forest, field, open arena) is as a rule simple obedience, useless in its essence, lacking true concentration and desire to learn.

87

Ill. 27. Schooling in the manege

Aside from her external, purely "behavioral" attention, a horse has what may be called "myological attention", when every tendon and every fascia of her body turns on and listens for your voice and the movements of your hands.

The bite of a horsefly, or a fly landing on the horse's stomach or hindquarters, a change in the wind, footing giving way under a hoof or no less than a thousand different circumstances will break the horse's precise equilibrium and destroy this "myological attention" completely.

XXXI

Any talk about the "naturalness" of work in fields or forests is the simple speech of a dilettante. It reveals their lack of knowledge about the intricacies of a horse's way of thinking, their lack of skill in a horse's education, and their lack of awareness of the way different "outside factors" influence horse biomechanics etc...

XXXII

Although it is very fashionable in these days, the word "naturalness" is unfortunately absolutely empty because it is not clear what it means in relation to a horse. There are no precise, intelligible criteria of "naturalness". The word "natural" refers to some sort of "primitive state" of conditions of existence.

Even here a primitive state is understood as something very positive.

By applying this logic to another creature, a human being, then we are led to believe that the best way to live is in a rudimentary form of existence, and the most comfortable habitats are those that were typical during the times of Pithecanthropus or even better, the Neanderthal man.

This "naturalness", in its essence is a poor substitute for a horse's true freedom.

XXXIII

A pseudo-herd, i.e., natural herd management is not "freedom" in any sense of the word, and only leads to the mental and physical degradation of a horse, turning the horse's life into a world of primitive relations and forming typical, almost primordial myology in the horse.

The myological features of a horse that appear when the horse is a member of a primitive-style herd are by themselves not bad and aren't destructive for a horse, but they are developed for an absolutely different style of movement than the style of the School.

Under the influence of "natural herd" life everything in a horse changes. Her physiology becomes highly economical, and any "School" movements create irritation in the horse because the muscles that make these movements possible are not important to the "primitive" life style.

Those muscles quickly dystrophy and the strongest muscles become ones that are less important for any of the School movements.

XXXIV

Of course, for photo sessions, filming or any other similar reason, work outside of a manege is possible, but only as an exception. I would recommend to avoid them and to obey the old, strict School rule that prescribes teaching the basic lessons only in a manege.

7. Elements

XXXV

Here it is possible to analyze several movements that perfectly exercise the horse. (On the condition that spatium and all the School interdicts are kept.)

The entire education of a horse in the School way is specifically based (and has always been based) on the very difficult elements. Difficult elements have a secret as well.

The secret is contained in the fact that they are not difficult at all — these are natural horse movements during moments of ardour, rage or fear. The School practice of work in hand and at liberty begins its teaching of so called difficult elements almost at the very beginning of the education of a horse.

Pesade, Spanish walk, passage, centavo, sentado, balancer, etc., fulfill a very important task — they all teach a horse voluntary concentration.

XXXVI

Teaching the elements of the School has one more secret: some sort of common business appears between a horse and human, it is a laborious task that takes a lot of time to solve, which has a "prologue, development, climax" form. This process has many elements, all of which must be developed. This process is reminiscent of a series of novels and thus manege discipline is automatically generated*.

---

* Regardless of the fact that most of the pictures that illustrate this part of "Tractate on a School Mount" are taken in a park, you should not conclude that teaching should be accomplished OUTSIDE OF A MANEGE, by the way.

Actually, the entire process of education and training of a horse must occur in a manege where there is ideal flatness and correct footing, where there are no flies, where the light is correct and nothing can distract a horse.

Of course, everything is based on a true relationship with a horse, on correct and absolutely gentle education, on thorough anatomical and physiological knowledge of a horse.

This mastery cannot become widespread of course, and an amateur cannot be allowed to work with the School horse.

I must add that a horse must not be used by the public, and only the School masters or those who profess the ideas of the School can be allowed to work with horses.

All the rest can satisfy their "love" for horses by collecting stamps or movies about horses.

XXXVII

I have already said that the basis of the School seat is an absolute absence of any fear of a horse. This is real knowledge of a horse.

XXXVIII

The best way to get rid of the natural, involuntarily spasm, which occurs in a human body as a response to quick and forceful movements of a horse, and as a consequence brings a person to confusion and uncertainty — is to practice high elements. The very best fit for this is the pesade (ill. 28).

XXXIX

With its power and height, with its energetic, forceful movement, which can seem extreme, — pesade, when performed correctly, helps to get rid of any natural and excusable fear, that must be felt by human's body lifted high above the ground and trusted to another creature.

XL

I am reminding you that PESADE — is the energetic, forceful movement that is perceived as correct only when a horse begins the upward movement in the front part of it's body, leaving the hind legs almost completely relaxed, instantly and consecutively engaging the muscles beginning always from the semitendinous muscle and up to the caudal part and through to the longissimus then down the leg to the medial head of the gastrocnemius muscle.

91

XLI

In the tradition of the School, the correct PESADE is the one during which the occipital bone goes strictly in and a little forward and the front legs are firmly bent in the carpal joint.

Of course, a horse must be fully gymnasticized at liberty (ill. 29), and taught to hold his balance almost vertically to the ground during even the most rapid lifts (table C).

The horse's health and her myological state must be irreproachable (ill. 30).

This is something a horse is taught during School games.

Then follows the teaching of CENTAVO (table D). In the illustration it is clear how disciplined and accurate the horse moves on its hind legs, maintaining balance and discipline.

XLII

Special consideration of a horse's vision has to be taken into account naturally as well. We must remember that the blind spot for her, above the occiput is always perceived as dangerous and worrying to the horse.

The School method during which at first a lift into a small pesade is done in a forest, under trees with dense and thick, but soft and almost stickless foliage (ill. 31). After going into a correct pesade and touching the occiput into thick foliage hanging above, a horse gains (once again) absolute confidence in the friendly nature of your requests. Besides this, it learns to lift in exactly the correct way without any fear for the poll and to go up straight with a flexed poll, which is required during a correct pesade and then in the courbette (a jump on hind legs).

← Ill. 28. Pesade
Ill. 29. "EQUILIBRIUM"   →

93

tab. C   *Equilibrium*

Phase *I*

Phase *II*

Phase *III*

Phase *IV*

Phase I

Phase II

Phase III

Phase IV

Correct practice of the School seat does not expect a rider to attempt to grip on to a horse with the legs during pesade. Leg placement is clearly seen on ill. 32.

XLIII

The most "forceful", and at the same time, energetic exercise, is the Caracole.

This name is an old School one; in the first centuries of the School's existence, it meant a very short, very collected powerful gallop, the most effective of all the gallops.

Ill. 30. Myological state of the School horse

The origin of the element's name is very simple — it came from a French verb "caracoler." It is true that back then this word, both silly and off the point, was used in the cavalry where it meant "shooting a horse from its place". Polemologists, perhaps because of the beauty of this word and misunderstanding of its meaning, also called it an incredibly foolish maneuver and thus it was laughed away by the contemporaries (General Krusso) and descendants (Sir Charles Oman).

Ill. 31. Lifting into a pesade in the forest ▶

96

In the School understanding CARACOLE is a manege gallop-like movement with maximum lifting of front legs and very soft mobilization of the caudal part at the same time.

Ill. 32. Position of rider's feet during pesade

The advantage of CARACOLE is in its deliberateness and "shortness" and that is why the gluteal profundus and the semitendinosus muscles, which feel the special strain, have a possibility to "breathe" after each half-tempo of caracole.

All four phases of the CARACOLE are shown in photos in table E.

XLIV

One of the most important elements was and probably will always be the Spanish walk, which exercises the trapezius muscles superbly.

Notably, if in exercising the trapezius there is (let's confess) an artificiality, then take into account the necessity of special toning up of all the near and under-saddle regions. The Spanish walk is not just feasible, but also dogmatically required (table F).

The same important element of exercising if also Piaffe (table F).

98

MAGNITUDO
Caracole

Caracole

tab. F

MAGNITUDO
Spanish Step

MAGNITUDO
Piaffe

(Precisely Piaf, and not "piafféeee", though strictly speaking, this manner of spelling and pronunciation is incorrect and is just School jargon. However, sacred School jargon is better than a vapid correctness.)

Nevertheless, despite the need and importance of piaf, passage, and of Spanish walk in exercising, in MAGNITUDO, in revelation, and education of the School mount's power; CARACOLE rests as a king of the elements.

XLV

Generally speaking, it is the dilettantes who divide horses' movements into natural and artificial.

That funny distinction was introduced by sports dressage, ideologists of whom are the keepers and prophets of principled hippological ignorance, and this distinction found further lodgment in their minds thanks to FEI rules, which are concentrated forms of barbarism, lies and hypocrisy.

What does real, official, hyppological science think about it?

A famous work of G. Waring (*Horse Behavior*), which systematized all the currently known knowledge about natural horse behavior, and which has the status of a textbook, maintains an absolutely different position than that of the FEI.

It is enough just to open the book, and on the 48th page, in the detailed description list of all the native, natural movements of the horse, we'll see – Ballotade, Capriole, Courbette, Croupade, Levade, Mezair, Sentado, etc.

G. Waring confines himself to affirmation and summation of the facts, observations, and scientific research. It is clear that he shows extremely authoritative evidence.

However, for the School there hasn't ever been a question about "artificiality" of elevated, high elements.

The key question still remains as to "WHY?"
Why did you mount? Why did you appear astride a horse?
The question is merciless, uncomfortable, but without an answer to which a seat will never become the School seat.

www.ingramcontent.com/pod-product-compliance
Lightning Source LLC
Chambersburg PA
CBHW061704120626
46550CB00003B/1076